DATE DUE			
FEB 7			
FEB 21			
NOV 8			
MAR 26			
FEB 17			
SEP 2			
OCT 23			
1/16/89			
1/17/89			
JA 29 '02			
GAYLORD			

STORY OF

THE NEGRO

In this account of the history of his people, Arna Bontemps has told the story that, he says, "I would have given my eye teeth to know when I was a high school boy in California—the story that my history books scarcely mentioned."

Its scope is wide. The rich and colorful picture of the Negro in Africa is background for what was to follow: the boatloads of stolen men brought to the shore of America to be sold as slaves. The long, hard struggle that ensued is a story filled with courage and heroism. What adventure stories can rival the tales of the slave ships *Le Rodeur* and the *Saint Leon;* the mutiny of the *Amistad* captives; the insurrection of the Haitian slaves; the accounts of the escapes via the Underground Railroad?

Mr. Bontemps introduces a long and varied procession of heroes, such as the blessed Martín de Porres of old Lima, Peru; Phillis Wheatley, the slave girl poet who charmed Boston and London; the orator Frederick Douglass; the educator Booker T. Washington; and the scholar and writer, W.E.B. Du Bois.

But aside from the drama that fills every chapter, there is an inherent dignity through the book—the dignity of a people fighting for freedom.

STORY OF
THE NEGRO

by ARNA BONTEMPS

Illustrated by Raymond Lufkin

FOURTH EDITION

New York : Alfred · A · Knopf

325.2

To

LANGSTON HUGHES

Published April 26, 1948
Reprinted four times
Second Edition, November 1955
Third Edition, February 1958
Reprinted two times
Fourth Edition, January 1964
Second Printing, April 1964

The Negro Speaks of Rivers

I've known rivers:
I've known rivers ancient as the world and older than the
    flow of human blood in human veins.

My soul has grown deep like the rivers.

I bathed in the Euphrates when dawns were young.
I built my hut near the Congo and it lulled me to sleep.
I looked upon the Nile and raised the pyramids above it.
I heard the singing of the Mississippi when Abe Lincoln
    went down to New Orleans, and I've seen its
    muddy bosom turn all golden in the sunset.

I've known rivers:
Ancient, dusky rivers.

My soul has grown deep like the rivers.

—LANGSTON HUGHES

Contents

The Ship   3

Men of the Lakes

    Short Africans   11
    . . . and Tall   16
    The Oldest Nation   20
    The Golden Prairies   26
    Timbuctoo   31

The Crossing

    Looking Back   39
    Man-Hunters   47
    The *Rainbowe*   53
    Slave Ships   57
    The Harbor of Le Cap   62
    The Coachman of Bréda   72
    Eighth Wonder of the World   78

The Bondage

    New People   87
    America's Crispus Attucks   91
    Phillis Wheatley's America   97

Freedom Is a Powerful Word   108
Free Men of Color   116
Masters and Slaves   122
Voices   127
The Star   134
Four Who Fled   140
The *Amistad*   147
Battle Hymn   155

Making a New World

The Disappointment   163
Beginning Again   171
Working with the Hands   176
The Talented Tenth   185
Awakening   194
The Test   208

Chronology   219

Index   235

The Ship

The Ship

THE story begins with a mystery—a ship without a
name. It flew the Dutch flag and had the appearance
of an armed trader, but that doesn't say much. Appear-
ances were not to be trusted at sea in 1619. The vessel
may have been sailing under false colors. She may just as
well have been a slave ship or a privateer. Whatever her
name or nation, however, her deeds are known and recorded.

This is the ship that brought the stolen Africans to the
young colony at Jamestown.

It was a summer day. The breeze along the Virginia coast was too small and weak to whiten the caps of waves. In the sky overhead seagulls dipped and swooped in vain. The fish they sought had descended to the cooler depths. The nameless ship wallowed in sluggish swells. With every yard of sail up, her progress was still slow. And perhaps there was grumbling on board.

Certainly the crew had reason to murmur. A voyage which must have promised rip-roaring adventures, taverns by the waterfront and orange trees in the tropics was coming to a shabby end. Provisions were gone, the water was low, and the stench that came out of the vessel's hold was unbearable. A hundred near-dead creatures were there, tortured by chains and gasping for food and drink. They were human slaves captured from a Spaniard. But there is no reason to think that the shame and wretchedness of such a cargo disturbed the crew of this ship. If there was grumbling above deck, it was for other reasons. Nowhere on board could a man get a breath of cool fresh air.

At first the colonists at Jamestown were alarmed by the approaching vessel. Was it a Spanish ship coming to attack them for daring to settle on land which was claimed by the king of Spain? If so, they were in a bad way. They had no adequate defense against the double rows of cannon which they saw sticking out of the advancing gunports. All they could do was to take a tighter grip on their muskets, whisper a few prayers and wait.

As the ship drew nearer, the fears of the settlers were gradually allayed. They saw on closer inspection that the cannons were not being rolled out and that none of the crew was armed. When the stranger ran up a Dutch flag, they felt completely reassured. Soon the captain was ashore, standing harmlessly among them but presenting an awkward proposition. In exchange for provisions the captain of the mystery ship offered *men*. Men of Africa, capable black men torn from their homes in another world, captured and re-captured and now offered in exchange for the food and water that a ship's famished crew requires—surely the Jamestown colonists could use some more strong hands to help them slay the trees of the New World, till the unbroken earth and beat back the tribes of the forest.

Of course, they could. In a new world—any new world—nothing is so important as strong men. In a new colony or settlement struggling to take root and live on the shores of a new land, nothing counts like men. Pioneers who have their work cut out for them don't need to be told the value of men. Those at Jamestown were no different from others in this respect. But there was one important difference. The original settlers at Jamestown had no intention of practicing slavery—not at this date, in any case.

There was among them, to be sure, a system of indentured servitude brought over from England. Under this system and according to their habit the services of a person could be obtained by another under certain con-

ditions and for a period of time. It was not an unlimited
bondage like slavery. It was not full ownership of one
person by another, and it was not an hereditary condition extending to the children of the indentured ones.
This was the system they knew at Jamestown, and it was
with something like this in mind that they listened to the
captain of the nameless ship and finally made a deal. A
few years later the relationship between the settlers and
their dark servants degenerated into ordinary slavery.

When the deal was closed that August day at Jamestown, twenty Negroes were taken from the hold of the
strange ship and left to do the bidding of the colonists in
return for provisions which the settlers were able to supply the vessel and its crew. Then without further ado the
ship was on its way again. Where did it go? And what
became of the rest of the stolen cargo, the other eighty
Negroes taken from the Spaniard?

The answers can only be guessed, but it is better to
ask still another question first. What were the Spaniards
going to do with the captured Africans if the nameless
Dutch vessel hadn't interfered? Maybe they were headed
for one of Spain's island possessions. Spain had maintained a colony in the new world for nearly a century before the English landed at Jamestown, and slavery was
not new to the Spaniard. Moreover, slavery has always
been a grim business.

It isn't worth while to try to follow the stranger that
stopped at Jamestown. All trace of the ship is lost, but
perhaps it is natural to suppose that the other eighty

Negroes perished at sea. On a vessel that was short of provisions, it was generally those below decks who went hungry. If in this case eighty out of one hundred died, it would not have been considered unusual in the trade of a slaver.

But this is not the story of the eighty who were lost. It is the story of the twenty who were landed. To this small group of captives, sad and tired and sick with longing for their own homes, Jamestown was not the beginning of a story. To them it was just the end of a chapter.

Men of the Lakes

Short Africans

THE trembling captives who stood before the settlers on the Virginia coast and the thousands of others like them who were brought to the New World in the next two centuries were not born slaves. Neither were they indentured servants. In their own land some of them were herdsmen and metal workers, others were hunters and boatmen, a few were warriors and princes, linguists and historians, storytellers and sculptors, painters, poets and musicians. Africa was their home and that is where their story begins.

The dark years of slavery were just an episode in the whole history of these people.

The important thing to remember is that the people of Africa are not all the same. Not all of them are of the same color and not all are the same size. All do not speak the same language or like the same food or wear the same clothes. There are more kinds of people, more languages, more separate countries in Africa than there are in Europe. And there are greater differences among Africans than among the peoples of Europe. In Africa one can find examples not only of the lightest and darkest races, but also of the tallest and shortest ones.

Consider the pygmies, for instance. Because they have been prisoners of the forest for so many centuries, dwelling among the great trees in the depths of the jungle, they have remained during most of this time a mystery and a legend to the rest of the world. In the third chant of the *Iliad* Homer, the poet of ancient Greece, speaks of storks that flew over the sea to wage bloody battles with the tiny men called pygmies. Homer had noticed, no doubt, that the storks migrated each year from Europe to Africa. Either his own bright imagination or the tall tale of some contemporary traveler was responsible for the amazing story of combat between these marauding birds and a race of small people inhabiting the African wilderness. It still makes a good story, even though it no longer seems like a true one, but the important thing it reveals is that the ancient Greek poet knew something about the pygmies and where they lived.

Of course, he was not the only writer of early times to show an interest in these curious little folk. The philosopher Aristotle, one of the most learned men of the ancient world, mentioned the pygmies as dwelling somewhere near the sources of the Nile river. At least two early Roman writers, Pliny and Pomponius Mela, had something to say about them, but Pliny added the suggestion that pygmies also existed in other parts of the world. In this he was quite correct, for there are still pygmies in parts of Asia, and also in some of the islands of the Pacific.

In the courts of the pharaohs pygmies of the forest were in great demand, somewhat as dwarfs were in the courts of medieval kings in Europe. Egyptian rulers sent expeditions into the mysterious region of "shade land" near the equator to capture and bring back the small folk.

A letter from a pharaoh to one of his officers more than three thousand years before Christ tells how the officer, who had come across the pygmy in the course of his explorations, sent the little fellow as a present to the king. The king was so pleased by the gift that he wrote a letter of thanks and the officer was so flattered by the king's letter that he had it engraved on the wall of his tomb. That is how it happened to be preserved.

About seventy years later Heru Khuf, another army officer of ancient Egypt, was sent by Pepi II into the "land of great trees" far away to the southward with orders to fetch another of those pygmies, alive and in good health. Whether or not the early Egyptian pharaohs considered the presence of pygmies good luck, as the rulers of medieval Europe believed about the dwarfs of their courts, is not too clear, but there is no doubt that they would go to some trouble to get one.

Unfortunately for the pygmies, the other peoples of Africa never quite shared the Egyptians' sentimental feeling. Larger and stronger tribes of the interior always drove the tiny ones from the high lands where the weather was most agreeable and from the open spaces where plantain and banana trees grew. The pygmy had to retreat into the tangled heart of the Congo jungle and to make his living by hunting and fishing. He became an expert in the use of the bow and arrow. He became equally skillful in the use of the spear, and he learned to make a serviceable shield by plaiting bark. He also seems to have known all the tricks of trapping.

In appearance, too, the pygmy is an interesting little person. Because so much of his life is spent under the leafy canopy of the jungle, his skin is not black. It ranges in shade from yellow to coffee brown. He is about four and a half feet high and has small elegant hands with attractive fingernails. His feet are likewise small and neatly formed, but usually they turn inwards enough to give him a slightly pigeon-toed look.

Some of the anthropologists have said that the pygmies belong to "an original race" which made its home in central Africa and in southern Asia long before the present races penetrated those regions. Whether this is true or not, there is certainly a world of difference between these ancient and intriguing little people and the magnificient Watussi, Africa's tallest and most beautiful people today.

. . . and Tall

THE modern world first heard about the Watussi at the beginning of the present century when the explorer Count Gustav Adolf von Goetzen made his way across the mountain barriers that surround the country of these unusual people. It is not hard to imagine with what astonishment the Count made his discovery, for this was a nation of dark princes whose men were not only elegant and slender but beautifully garbed as well. What's more they were from seven to eight feet tall.

It may be true, as one anthropologist has said, that the

Watussi are the descendants of rich cattle owners of upper Egypt who, once upon a time, migrated from the empire of the pharaohs. Whether they moved to escape famine or strife or to seek greener pastures for their prize herds or just for adventure makes little difference now. The important point is that their journey brought them around Lake Victoria to Rwanda, a region in central Africa where the climate is moderate and healthful, where the soil is rich and the countryside beautiful, where the neighboring inhabitants are gentle and friendly.

If that is indeed their early history, as some who have made a study of their customs, traditions, superstitions and taboos believe, then it is not hard to understand why the neighboring tribes in that section of the Congo were so impressed. To the meek, peace-loving Bahutu, five feet tall and not dressed very well, the lordly and beautiful Watussi looked like a god. To the knee-high pygmies, even more so. As a result eighty thousand Watussi men of today are princes, governors, nobles and chiefs, ruling about three million lowly Bahutu farmers and herdsmen and being served by an uncounted number of Batwa pygmies who are the hunters, the bodyguards and the personal servants of the sculptured Watussi giants.

These towering men with their fine features and aristocratic ways are also remarkable athletes. Much time is spent in the cultivation of their bodies. Nothing delights the Watussi more than demonstrations of physical conditioning. The art he enjoys most is the dance, and the sport he prefers is high jumping. A Watussi prince starts practicing jumps at an age when an American boy would be learning soft ball. By the time he is grown he may be able to jump nearly eight feet. If he is outstanding, he will be invited to jump for the king.

If he has ability of another sort, the young Watussi may take a part in the Lion Dance and appear before the king with a group of performers who wear a lion's mane on their heads and bells on their ankles and dance to the rhythm of horns and native instruments. Graceful Watussi virgins, if they come from the best families and study dancing from infancy, may become members of a royal ballet attached to the court of the king. In this they will wear a belt and fringed skirt of antelope skin. Their dances will be delicate and chaste and unlike the dancing of less cultivated African people.

The Watussi is, of course, a gentleman farmer by profession, and his specialty is cattle. His way of life is built around the care and keeping of these superb animals, and his ideal of beauty is influenced by his admiration for the creatures. He even compliments his sweetheart by comparing her to a cow. To him the longest and most triangular face is the prettiest of all, and a double-horned headdress is very chic indeed.

The cows of these people are as remarkable as their owners. Apparently there are two important breeds of which one, called "the ones which were found," are considered the royal cows and the other, called "the cows with the long, long horns," are the sacred cows. The royal cows are believed to have been discovered by one of the first kings of the present dynasty. The sacred cows are remarkable for their horns, which often measure twelve or more feet from point to point.

Everything possible is done to keep the cows looking their best. All the milk is left to the calves except a small bit reserved for the herdsmen, who themselves belong to a tribe specially dedicated to the work. Ornaments of pearls and leaves and white flowers are made for the necks, heads, horns and tails of the animals. Frequently the cows are exhibited in colorful ceremonies.

To many people the Watussi are not only the tallest but the handsomest African people. To some the pygmies are the funniest as well as the shortest. In the whole story of the Negro, however, the interesting thing that both reveal is the great variety to be found among the people of Africa. Between these two extremes of size and culture are many ordinary Africans. Each has his own language and his own history. And while this is not the place to include every one of them, perhaps a few should be mentioned.

The Oldest Nation

THE Ethiopians are among the African people who have the longest history.

The ancient Egyptians called the land of the Ethiopians Kush. The Greeks called it Ethiopia. We call it Ethiopia. And if we need any extra proof that Ethiopia has existed as a nation for two thousand or more years, we can find it in the writings of the Greek poet Homer who mentioned it in his *Iliad*, written in the ninth century before Christ. Homer said that Zeus and other gods went each year to a twelve-day feast among the "blameless Ethiopians."

The Greek historian Herodotus described the Ethiopians of his day as "the tallest and handsomest and longest-lived of men." He said of their country that it extended "farthest of inhabited lands to the southwest" and that it had "a great deal of gold, enormous elephants, all kinds of forest trees, including ebony."

The life-span of these men was said to have been one-hundred-and twenty years as contrasted with the eighty-year span claimed by their contemporaries in Persia, for example. And this was just one of many startling rumors that came out of the country in those days, based mainly on the story of the spies sent by Cambyses, King of the Persians. The spies also reported that the Ethiopians pulled bows of tremendous size, bound their captives in pure gold shackles and put their dead away in coffins made of transparent alabaster.

Cambyses refused to believe the tales and sent an army against the Ethiopians anyhow. But the invaders ran out of food and met disaster before they even approached the rich land.

The story that modern historians have pieced together is that five thousand or more years before Christ there flourished a Negroid empire in what is now the Anglo-Egyptian Sudan. This empire split into two parts, one Egyptian and one Ethiopian. After the breakup there was a period in which neither country made much progress, but about three hundred years later the two empires began to take shape.

The Egyptians, a mixed people who would be considered mulattos by American definition, moved ahead faster than the Ethiopians at first, but the black men got their chance later. This came as a result of the invasion of Egypt by barbarous tribes known as Hyksos. When the Hyksos overran their nation, many Egyptians fled into the land of their Ethiopian cousins for refuge. This was particularly true of the rulers, the scholars and the leading people. Many of the royal families of Egypt and Ethiopia intermarried during this period, and the result was that a member of one of these Egypto-Ethiopian families eventually raised an army of Ethiopian soldiers and liberated Egypt.

According to Herodotus, Ethiopian soldiers of that era went to war "clothed in leopard and lion skins. They had bows made of the stems of palm-leaves at least four cubits in length and long arrows of reed at the end of which was, instead of iron, a pointed stone which they also used for carving their seals. Besides this, they carried javelins armed with the horns of antelopes, pointed and worked like an iron lance head and clubs full of knots. When they went into battle, they rubbed half their body with chalk and the other half with vermilion."

In time the Egyptian star began to rise again. Then began a series of efforts to make Ethiopia a part of the Egyptian empire. Frequently Egypt sent armies, but never was she able to completely overcome Ethiopia. In

730 B.C., however, Ethiopia conquered Egypt and ruled that country for about a century. During that period Ethiopia took on Egyptian civilization.

Then as time passed some Semitic folk from the East migrated into Ethiopia. So many different kinds of people met and mingled there, in fact, that the Arabs started calling the inhabitants Abyssinians, a word which in Arabic means mixed people, and by this name the Ethiopians have been called for the past three thousand years.

About three centuries and a half after Christ the influence of His teachings began to reach Ethiopia from Europe, and by A.D. 530 enough of its people had been converted to cause the rest of the world to look upon this ancient empire as a Christian country. Of course, the way of the Christian is beset by trials and tribulations, as all Christians know, and Ethiopia's experiences with the new religion were not exceptional. Hers began when an unfriendly princess of the Axumite kingdom in Arabia stood on her throne and ordered all Ethiopians out of the realm. Naturally this led to hard feelings, and the result was that Ethiopia soon found herself surrounded by enemies and cut off from the rest of the world. She remained isolated for nearly a thousand years.

One of the romantic results of this long isolation was the legend of Prester John. During all those centuries when there was no news out of Ethiopia the outside world forgot the little it knew about the country. Rumor and gossip took the place of real information, and word went around that an amazing king ruled a fabulously

rich Christian kingdom in the heart of Africa. This great
king, the legend said, was so humble and so filled with
the true spirit of Christianity that he refused all pre-
tentious titles and called himself simply Prester John.
The search for this rich kingdom and its benign ruler
continued many years.

Meanwhile Christianity and Mohammedanism fought
hard in Ethiopia as elsewhere in Africa. At one time dark
Nubians from the upper Nile country, under the leadership of Christian-hating Romans, won control of the
country, but very soon the conquerors were conquered—
the Nubians themselves were converted to Christianity
and promptly took a hand in defending Ethiopia from
militant Mohammedanism. For two centuries they held
off the enemy by force of arms. Then for six more centuries they kept the Arab at bay by paying him tribute.
But Ethiopia was saved.

In more recent times the greatest threats to this ancient
kingdom have come from Europe. In 1896 Italy marched
against the old nation with the intention of adding it to
her empire. But the Ethiopians were strong enough to
turn the enemy back, and the invading army was badly
beaten. So humiliating was the defeat, in fact, that Benito
Mussolini, a generation later, made a second invasion of
Ethiopia the most important event on his calendar in
1935. This time, with bombs and poison gas and modern
machines of war, the result was different. The proud,
painted warriors of Africa's oldest independent nation
were out of date and no trouble at all to the men in tanks

and airplanes. The king fled to England, and Ethiopia was occupied by the armies of Italy.

Of course that was not the end. A war in Europe followed the rape of Ethiopia; this war went against the forces of Mussolini, and that ruler was defeated and overthrown.

Haile Selassie, the exiled king of Ethiopia, a modern day Prester John in some ways, returned to his throne with the help and support of enlightened people everywhere, and Ethiopia turned over a new page of history.

The Golden Prairies

TWO large Negro nations and perhaps ten smaller ones grew between the Atlantic Ocean on the west and the Red Sea on the east. At the time of their greatest expansion both the Songhay and the Mandingo empires were as large as the present United States. Each had a history that went back beyond the founding of the British Empire.

When the world was young and beautiful, men with gleaming black bodies came from the lake country in the East. They had met and conquered the lion, the gorilla, the wild elephant and every other jungle enemy. But they couldn't possibly have guessed to what wonderous places and what strange experiences that happy, careless march through the grass of the forest would finally lead.

Years later other adventurers came from the lake country. These men who followed in this second migration may have been even more eager and energetic than the first, for they worked out new methods of farming. They started raising cattle and poultry. They domesticated the guinea-fowl. They learned from others how to make fire, and they began using it to cook food. They invented the working of iron and the making of pottery.

Some of these Negroes from the region of the African lakes thrashed through the tall grass to the edges of the Sahara and the banks of the Niger. There they met and mingled with Berbers, men of the desert, and with Semitic nomads from Arabia. When they settled down, history began in the empires of Ghana, Melle and Songhay.

The empire of Ghana goes back at least as far as A.D. 300, perhaps earlier. In a book called *Golden Prairies,* whose Arabian author died in 956, Ghana's capital is described and some of its history traced. Under a dynasty of black kings it reached its greatest power and development and ruled over the veiled Zenaga people and the Berbers of the desert. About 1050 Ghana began to decline, and two centuries later it fell before the conquering Mandingo armies.

Meanwhile, beginning around A.D., 600, another State

was founded on the western stretches of the Niger. At
first its territory was limited to the islands in the river
and the territory along its west bank. Little by little it
grew, and finally it extended all the way to Timbuctoo,
which was later to become the capital city and the cultural and commercial center of this great Songhay empire.

The Songhay, however, did not always have things
their own way. A strong rival rose up in the west and
established a capital at Jenne, the city which was eventually to give its name to the Gulf of Guinea and the whole
Guinea coast. This was the empire of the Mandingo,
sometimes called Melle, which fought the Songhay across
the centuries in the manner of European States, pushing
one another back and forth from generation to generation.

In general what happened in the African nations of
the middle ages was influenced by world events and the
trends of history as a whole. For example, powerful
Carthage on the southern shore of the Mediterranean
stood between Africa and Europe until 146 B.C. In that
year the conquest of Carthage by Rome was completed,
and the Romans took over in North Africa. These newcomers immediately went to work at their favorite hobby
—building roads. They also set up libraries and schools
and did whatever else they could to spread the Roman
empire beyond the Mediterranean. And not only did they
take in most of Egypt and the area north of the Sahara

but some of their generals crossed the desert, went into the Sudan and explored the fertile basin of the Niger.

Then in 476 the Roman Empire fell, and the connection between Africa and Europe was broken. For a thousand years Africa was left undisturbed by western powers, and during this period the great West African civilizations of Ghana and Songhay and Mandingo grew and flourished. Meanwhile, a mighty force of another kind swept into Africa from the east.

This was the beginning of the Mohammedan conquest. The swarthy Arab armies of a fighting religion rode into northern Africa for the first time in the seventh century after Christ. On their beautiful pitch-black horses, with the crescent and the sword as their shining symbol, they overran all the country between the Red Sea and the Atlantic Ocean. Then in 718 they crossed the Strait of Gibraltar, entered Spain and overthrew the Visigoth rulers of that land. They remained in Spain as its conquerors for the next four hundred years, and during these years much happened.

The armies of the Moors were constantly replenished with fighting men from Africa; all of these were dark, and many were black. The result was that a strong trace of Africa was left forever on the peoples of the Spanish peninsula. That Latin type of beauty, sometimes so highly favored, can be traced to the mingling that followed this invasion. African culture, too, put a mark on Spain in these years. Spanish music and Spanish dancing took on some of the warm rhythms of Negro Africa.

Christian warriors reconquered part of Spain in the eleventh century, but another four hundred years passed before the last of the Mohammedans were driven back into Africa.

Timbuctoo

WHEN the Moors were driven out of Spain, they returned to Morocco. Their old homeland had changed greatly. The most important change was that now the rulers of the country were Arab invaders. While the Moors were away fighting and ruling Spain, Arabs from the east had come in and conquered Morocco.

The only thing the defeated homecomers could do now was to lead their armies farther south. So it was down the Atlantic coast that they went, finally becoming nomads in the Negro countries and wandering about the lakes on the left bank of the Niger and in the neighborhood of Timbuctoo. To make sure that everybody would know who they were and where they came from, they called themselves Andalusians, and they have continued to call themselves by that name ever since.

Among these Moors and the no-nation folk who came with them from Spain were many men of talent and distinction. Some were architects who had built palaces and mosques in Seville, Granada and Cordova. With their herds of goats and humped oxen, with their flocks of sheep and their horses, they also brought along some books. The delicate ornamentation of their leather work, their embroidered wallets, their cushions and gun cases, like their fine jewelry, reflected the rich life they had lived as the masters of Spain. These were the Moors who marched on Timbuctoo in 1591.

They found the city to be, like Jenne and Gao and other cities of central Africa at that time, as advanced in trade as it was in scholarship and in the art of gracious living. Its main wealth was in salt and gold dust, but the workshops of the city were never able to supply the demand for the white embroidered robes for which Timbuctoo was famous. These lovely creations had roses and arabesques worked on the back and front in bright threads that stood out in shiny whiteness from the raw silk of the fabric. The people of Gao and of Bammaku and of far Morocco could never get as many of them as they wanted.

Timbuctoo's leather work was also wanted. Its shops

turned out boots decorated with green and yellow embroidery and slippers and cushions that were just right for floors covered with soft carpets and panther skins. And it dealt in mirrors and needles, seed pearls for embroidery work and large ones for necklaces, silk and perfumes, teapots and snuffboxes, dates and cloves, tea and coffee, carpets, paper, cups and a dozen other commodities. Great lines of camels, loaded with articles of this kind, followed the long caravan routes across the Sudan, to Mossi and the region of Lake Chad.

A merchant fleet of river boats operated on the Niger and transported cargoes of millet, rice, honey, nuts, flour, monkey-bread, tamarinds, onions, tobacco, dried fish, soap, iron, cotton, potteries and calabashes to smaller villages and towns along the river. To Morocco and the cities of the north they carried gold, ivory, ostrich plumes, raw leather, wax, incense, musk, gum, indigo and sometimes slaves.

The University of Sankoré, which the Moors found at Timbuctoo, was known all over Africa. Learned men and scholars came to it from Morocco, Tunis and Egypt. Sometimes its own professors journeyed to Fez, Cairo, Bagdad and even Granada to exchange ideas with professors in the universities of those cities. More than once the Mohammedan histories tell how these Negro scholars "astounded the most learned men of Islam by their erudition." Some of them were kept as regular professors both in Morocco and Egypt, as was also the Negro Juan Latino at the University of Granada in Spain somewhat later.

While Africa as a whole was largely unexplored, the city of Timbuctoo was known so well in Europe that a Catalan map maker included it on a map dated 1373.

The libraries of Timbuctoo were famous. Much of the material in them concerned the Prophet whose religion the people had accepted, but there were also many books on history, medicine, astronomy and poetry. Timbuctoo was known as a city that loved books. The manufacture and sale of them became one of the important businesses.

Fortunately, not all the books of Timbuctoo have perished. Of these the most important is perhaps the *Tarikh es Soudan.* This great chronicle of the countries of the Niger was written by a Negro scholar who was a studious but dreamy-eyed boy at the time that the nameless ship dropped its strange cargo at Jamestown. The name of that historian was Abderrahman Sadi el Timbucti. He was the son of parents who were themselves lovers of poetry and science as well as being very religious people, and his great teacher was Ahmed Baba, author of 20 known books. Sadi became secretary to an official of high rank in the government. In this capacity he traveled a great deal and lived sometimes at Timbuctoo and sometimes at Jenne, a city of almost equal prominence, but wherever he went and whatever else he did, he never neglected the great book he was writing. His ambition was to write a complete history of all the countries of the Niger.

His position gave him access to all the letters and

papers that existed in the African cities of his day, and his voyages and journeys were of help too. "I have asked the help of God," he says in his introduction, "in writing down all that I have read, seen, or heard concerning the kings of the Sudan and the Songhay people, and in relating their history and the events connected with their expeditions of war. I shall speak of Timbuctoo and of its foundation, of the princes who have wielded the power of that city, I shall mention the learned and pious men who dwelt therein, and I shall continue this history to the close of the dominion of sultans of Morocco."

All that he attempted he accomplished. The book he produced, next to the holy writings, became the favorite African volume. Its richness and flavor and the way in which it brings the past to life have led some scholars to say that it does for the people of the Sudan what the writings of Homer and Herodotus do for ancient Greece, what Froissart's *Chronicles,* from which Shakespeare got much of his historical material, do for the people of France.

Yet the *Tarikh* was only one of the histories of the Sudan. An even earlier work was called the *Fatassi.* Its author was Mohaman Koti, a Negro author born thirty-two years before the discovery of the New World. A later history, the title of which is translated as the *Divan of Kings,* tells events between 1656 and 1747 in the Sudan. But while its author was writing about the pomp and luxury of dark rulers and recording their wars and conquests and family trees, history of another kind was being made along the Gulf of Guinea, sometimes known as the Gold Coast, the Grain Coast, the Ivory Coast, but from that time on as the Slave Coast.

Out there the men with chains had arrived.

The Crossing

Looking Back

THE story of human slavery is almost as old as man. Egypt had slaves, as everyone who has read the Old Testament knows. Those who have read Homer's *Iliad* or *Odyssey* know that the ancient Greeks practiced slavery before the Trojan War. And in the time of Rome the custom of holding slaves became even more widespread than in earlier history.

When primitive man was just a hunter, he killed his enemy in a fight with clubs or stones and dragged the womenfolk off by the hair, no doubt. He had no use for the men he had beaten and hence did not make captives of them. In those days most of the work at home was done by women, and this created a demand for more and more female servants, as well as wives.

In the herdsman stage, a man could use a few slaves to help with the domestic animals. A few others could be sold. So, at that stage, primitive man captured some of his defeated enemies and killed the rest. As soon as man learned to work sitting down and to enjoy life by stretching out his feet in front of a fire, however, the need for somebody to hand him things, to run errands, to do the digging and the scuffling, and to clean up after the master began to be felt. That's when it occurred to him that it was silly to kill the defeated enemy. Why not bring him home and put him to work?

As time passed, careful systems were worked out to help in dealing with slaves and to make it easier for people to live in a community which included them. These systems or codes were not the same in all countries. In Greece, for example, slaves were less harshly treated than in some other slaveholding nations, both ancient and modern. There the slave had some protection before the law. If he were too cruelly treated, he could always run away and find refuge in the temples of the gods, before the altars, and in the sacred groves. He could testify against his master and demand to be sold if he could prove that the master had wronged him. In Rome, on the other hand, the master had the power of life and death over the slave.

From earliest times there has also been a great variety in the kinds of work done by slaves. In most cases, as one might expect, bondsmen were given the meanest and dirtiest jobs. Often, however, the opposite was true. In Athens there were twelve hundred Sythian archers, all of them slaves, whose duties appear to have been comparable to those of city policemen. Other slaves were flute players in the homes of the rich, and some of the females were dancing girls.

At least one slave was among the most gifted men of the ancient world. He called himself Aesop, a name which in Greek is the same as Ethiop, and in some ways he was like a classical Uncle Remus. But Aesop had a mind of great depth as well as wit, and he has had a powerful influence on the thought as well as the moral views of many of the greatest thinkers in history.

Not much is known about the early life of this famous slave. Few personal histories of slaves were ever kept anywhere. All masters of slaves must keep repeating a strange falsehood. They must convince themselves somehow that slaves are not human beings. Otherwise an unpleasant feeling of guilt will trouble the mind of the owner. That is why it is so hard to piece together the things one likes to know about interesting and gifted people, when they happen to have been slaves. About Aesop, we are told that he lived in the sixth century before Christ, that he came from Phrygia, and that his first master was named Xanthus.

Planudes the Great, a monk of the fourteenth century

A.D., the scholar who first presented the Fables of Aesop to the modern world, mentioned the slave's flat nose, his thick lips, and his black skin, but these negroid features had nothing to do with slavery as it was known and practiced in the ancient world. Slaves were of all nations and races in those days, and Greeks were generally preferred. Yet this description of Aesop gives him a rather special place in the story of the Negro, and it has caused coin experts to believe that the Negro head found on medals at Delphi was the head of the famous black slave.

Aesop was the man who first told the story about the frogs who wanted a king. These frogs, he said, found life in their pond dull, so they prayed to the god Jupiter, and Jupiter heard their prayers and sent them a big log with a great splash. This log would be their king. But after the first splash the log lay dead in the water. What kind of king was this? The frogs hopped on him with contempt. Again they prayed to Jupiter. They wanted a real king. This time he answered by sending a stork. After that the pond was no longer dull. The stork made life very exciting indeed—by eating the frogs.

At another time, Aesop observed that the Creator of man did not mix the clay with water, but instead used tears. Yet Aesop, we gather, was valued by his owner mainly as a house servant and a yard boy. More shocking still is the report that one of his stories so outraged the people of Delphi that they framed a false charge against him, had him captured by soldiers and thrown off a high cliff into the sea. According to the story, Aesop had been disappointed by what he found at this famous shrine and compared his feelings on seeing it to those of one who stands on a beach thinking he sees something of importance drifting ashore and discovers at last only a mass of seaweed and rubbish. The inhabitants of Delphi were afraid that this kind of talk would ruin their tourist business, and that seemed to them sufficient cause to hide a sacred cup in Aesop's luggage and later accuse him of stealing it.

But Aesop was not entirely without honor or recognition in his own day. He told one of his stories before Croesus, the rich King of Lydia, and so appealed to the monarch that Croesus let himself be persuaded not to invade Samos, as he had intended. Thereafter Aesop spent seven years in Lydia writing his *Fables,* and when he expressed a wish to travel, Croesus advanced him money as well as letters of introduction to the rulers of the East. The tours he took included Greece, Babylon, Egypt and a part of Asia. A high point of his travels was a banquet meeting with the Seven Wise Men of Greece at Corinth.

Perhaps Rome's most famous slave was the dramatist Terence, a native of Africa, purchased by Terentius Lucanus and later given freedom and a name by this rather exceptional master in recognition of the slave's genius. The comedies of Terence and his verses have been studied, admired and imitated for more than twenty centuries. The fact that Terence was called an *Afer* by

Latin writers and described as *fusco* in color has aroused the curiosity of some scholars interested in the achievement of Negroes of antiquity. The *Century Dictionary* says: "The ordinary terms for 'African negro' or 'African' were *Æthiops* and *Afer.*" *Fusco* may be translated as "very dark"—in contrast with *subfusco,* the word used to describe brownish, mulatto-type people like the Egyptians. Since slavery was not based on race in those times, however, it is hard to be definite about such questions.

Antar, known sometimes in Arab history as "Abul Fouaris" or "the father of heroes," was the harsh-featured, unattractive son of a black slave woman. Yet his place in the lore of the Mohammedan world has been compared to that of Roland in French history and Siegfried in the chronicles of Germany. Ignored by the wealthy chieftain who was his father and scorned by his humble mother, the young Antar was put to minding cattle. When a fight broke out among rival tribesmen over the possession of a famous mare called Jirwet, the fifteen year-old Antar threw himself into the battle and came out of it a hero. As a reward he was liberated from slavery by his father.

In later years Antar rose to the leadership of the Abs tribe. Other tribes laughed at the Abs for having a man who was not only a Negro but an ex-slave for their chief, but when he heard such remarks, Antar announced that he had a sword that was ready to challenge anyone who doubted the quality of his ancestry and blood. More than once during his romantic career, enemies and rivals made

Antar back up his proud words. The story of his life is as full of adventure, romance, and chivalry as any tale of knighthood.

More important than Antar's perils and conquests, though, was his literary genius. One of his poems is among the seven which hang at the entrance to the temple at Mecca, the highest honor a Moslem writer can receive. Some European critics have included him among the great poets of the world. A four-volume condensation of *The Romance of Antar* by Terrick Hamilton, was published in London in 1820, but there were earlier books about him in Germany and France, and Antar's own works have been published in Cairo in thirty-two volumes. The Russian composer Rimsky-Korsakoff based one of his best-known symphonies on the life and career of Antar and named it after the black hero.

Of course, not many slaves showed the genius of an Aesop, a Terence, or an Antar. There were as many kinds of slaves as there are kinds of people. But the humiliation of whips and chains was always the same. This kind of life debased both slave and master—the master more than the slave—and it made living miserable for the free laborer who went hungry while slaves did the work.

Another thing about slavery was universal, too. Once the system was introduced into a nation, it became necessary to replenish the number of slaves constantly. People in bondage never seemed to multiply fast enough to please their owners. For that reason the habit of kidnapping free people and selling them into slavery was common in all slave states. In ancient times, however, nations depended mainly on conquests of other countries to keep them supplied with slaves. After the Romans conquered all the world that seemed worth conquering in their day, including even the British Isles, one of the problems that bothered them was the growing inconvenience of having too few bondsmen and no place to look for more. When their nation fell apart, following invasions by tribes which the Romans called barbarian, there was still no way to make new slaves plentiful again, with the result that owners took special pains to hold those they had. This led to the system known as serfdom which took the place of slavery during the period between the fall of Rome and the discovery of the New World by Columbus.

Then came the task of founding overseas colonies. This was a particularly hard job, but the nations of western Europe found a way to make it much easier. They revived slavery.

Man-Hunters

THE first slaves in modern times were caught fifty years before Columbus made his discovery, but the number of captives remained small before colonization started and increased as the colonies grew. One depended on the other. All of the important New World settlements south of Plymouth, whether in North America, South America, or the islands of the Caribbean, depended on slave labor. The total debt of the New World to the sweat and blood of these forced workers has never been fully calculated.

The first modern slaver was perhaps Antam Gonsalves, a Portuguese officer somehow connected with the voyages of Prince Henry the Navigator. Here it must be recalled that the contacts between Negro Africa and Europe, such as existed when Rome ruled the lands bordering the Mediterranean, had been broken for a thousand years. The part of Africa which lies below the Sahara had grown dim and mysterious to outsiders. It was to explore this mystery that the sea-people of Portugal, encouraged by their adventurous Prince, sent ship after ship down the western coast. And when the men under Commander Gonsalves caught a fine-looking Moor wandering along the beach, they may have intended only to take him home as a sort of souvenir. It was the Moor, a young man of wealth and influence, who suggested that he could and would supply ten Negro boys in exchange for his own release. The deal was made, much to the satisfaction of Gonsalves. Not only was he glad to be getting ten for one but also, as he said, because "the ten blacks were not of the lineage of the Moors but were Gentiles and so the better to bring into the path of salvation." The things slave-catchers said to themselves to put their consciences at rest would make a book of marvels.

The ten youngsters were taken to Portugal where they became errand boys or house servants in the homes of rich families, and soon a demand for more African slaves was noticed. Nearly every ship that touched the Guinea coast thereafter picked up one or more young Negroes, both boys and girls, to take home to Portugal. Before long the vessels quit sailing on voyages of discovery and started thinking only of the profitable trade in human beings. To carry this on successfully the owners refitted many ships and built forts and stockades or factories on the African coast.

As the business grew, the Portuguese traders began selling people to Spain as well. A number of these Negroes and their descendants accompanied Spanish explorers on voyages across the Atlantic, and some of them are mentioned rather prominently in the chronicles and reports left by leaders of the expeditions.

A well-known example is Estevanico (Little Stephen), a member of a party of four which crossed the continent of North America in 1536, after a journey of nine years. Three years later Estevanico helped lead the first expedition into Arizona and New Mexico. He was killed by Zuni Indians who had received advance information about the ways of Spanish discoverers.

The companions of the explorers were probably not the first Negroes in the New World, however. There are many indications that Africans from the Guinea coast reached these shores before Columbus. Several Spanish documents mention Negro people found by Balboa and other conquerors when they first reached Panama. On the other hand, Mohammedan writings in Cairo speak of large boats undertaking voyages across the Atlantic from the Guinea coast as early as 1324. But this is another side of the story. We are concerned now with those Negroes who came as slaves.

A letter written by the governor of Haiti in 1503 shows that there were already a number of Negroes working in the island. This was just eleven years after Columbus's first voyage. It was one hundred and four years before the first colonists landed at Jamestown.

Englishmen like Sir John Hawkins were attracted to the slave business before there were British colonies with which to trade. Spanish settlements became their first customers. The French, the Dutch, and the Danes all handled some of the trade when the demand was great, but eventually the British did more of the slave business than all the other European nations put together. In one year the British caught, transported and sold 38,000 Africans, while the French were delivering 20,000, the Portuguese 10,000, the Dutch 4,000 and the Danes 2,000.

With the colonies in South America, the West Indies, and North America begging for strong black men and boys, well-favored women and girls, with the sailing fleets of European nations contending with one another for the business and sometimes fighting on the high seas, there was bound to be wild excitement along the Guinea coast. The big hunting season was on in Africa.

Often a whole village was surrounded at night. The slaver's men, armed with guns, would hide among the trees a safe distance away. Then one of their number would set fire to the sleeping village. As the frightened folk tried to escape the flames, they were caught by the slavers and hurried away to the factories near the beach. Offshore the ships were waiting.

How could pious Christian men like Commander An-tam Gonsalves and Sir John Hawkins descend to the wickedness of stealing human beings and selling them into slavery? How could they sleep with such black deeds on their minds?

Gonsalves, like many slavers brought up in the Catholic tradition, felt that he was really doing the Africans a favor by snatching them out of heathenism and giving them a chance to learn the true religion.

Men like Sir John worked under an even greater perplexity at first. As Englishmen and Protestants they were quite unfamiliar with slavery. They knew about indentured servants and they knew about free men, but what kind of people were slaves? They ended by deciding that slaves were not people at all. They were just property. And since all the slaves they knew at that time were black, they concluded that Negroes were not human beings and hence did not have to be treated according to the golden rule.

This was a strange notion, one which Shakespeare never heard in his lifetime, one which never once entered the heads of the Egyptians, the Greeks or the Romans, but Christian people of the slave era let themselves believe that it was no crime to rob Negroes of their wages, to cheat them of their rights or even their life.

This curious explanation took care of the worries of a great many people for a long time. It should always be remembered, however, that the best minds in England and in the United States, both Catholic and Protestant, refused to accept it. Most of the English poets and writers who saw how it worked, disapproved of slavery as well as of the weak excuses given for it. In the colonies the same was true. But not much attention was paid to these good people as long as the slave business continued to make money. Instead, the slavers became more and more brutal.

The Rainbowe

SLAVERY was practiced in Africa before the Europeans went into the business, but it was not the same then as it became afterward. Among the natives it was more like the ancient custom whereby the victor enslaved the enemy he had defeated in battle rather than put him to death. In this way it was considered an act of mercy. There were also in Africa, as in Greece and the ancient countries, definite conditions under which people might become slaves and also some by which they might gain freedom. Debt was frequently a cause, the understanding being that the individual would pay in labor what he had failed to pay in cash or goods. Bondage was sometimes the penalty for witchcraft. In still other cases, it was the punishment for disrespectful behavior toward another's religion or for becoming too friendly with a neighbor's wife.

Since slaves were generally treated like members of the family, these customs did not seem too severe. Nor did the Africans consider it very cruel to sell slaves under such conditions. In a time of famine or of great need, men would sell even wives or daughters without feeling that they had wronged these individuals. Of course, they were always reluctant to dispose of their sons.

This was the pattern of slavery when the first of the traders came from Europe, and nobody complained very much till things began to get out of hand. That is, until the demand for slaves and the profits from selling them became so great that the slavers started looking for ways to increase the supply. Then it was that they raised their offers to the native chiefs, causing the Africans to search harder for people to put on the block. Sometimes men were accused of witchcraft when their only crime was being young and strong—good material for the New World plantations. Other healthy young people who had been well-behaved all their lives were suddenly accused of disloyalty to the chief and hurried away into bondage. But all the slaves that could be obtained by such tricks were just a small part of the number the traders wanted. Still other methods had to be found.

Piracy and kidnapping soon took the place of buying and selling. When traders limited themselves to slaves already in bondage, slaves actually owned by African rulers and chieftains, their dealings were rather peaceful. The slaves accepted their lot meekly, expecting nothing worse than their present condition. When stealing and kidnapping became the rule, slavery turned into a nasty business.

Questions were asked no more. Anyone who brought a man or a woman down to the slave coast could depend on making a sale. Every bully and tough character in West Africa found a profitable occupation. All one had to do was to catch strangers in dark or shadowy places, tie them up securely, then deliver them at the water's edge. And since one act of violence generally brings on another, there was fighting and disorder all around. Large numbers of Negroes lost their lives resisting capture.

On the ships there was despair. Men of learning and fine skills were thrown into the ships with the rest. Sometimes a king came tumbling in after them. Baffled by all this, confused and hopeless, many of the slaves jumped overboard and drowned themselves in the sea. When the traders built high railings to restrain them, others refused to eat. But the slavers found that they could make a profit by delivering two out of every three, so the large number of suicides did not stop them.

Their answer was to outfit more and more slave ships. At one time there were almost a thousand of these horrible vessels sailing out of Liverpool alone. Soon ship owners of the English colonies were anxious to have a part in the profitable business. The *Rainbowe,* a vessel from Boston harbor, commanded by a Captain Smith, made the first recorded voyage for slaves by an American ship. The experience it met was nothing to flatter good Americans.

Just twenty-six years after the mystery ship landed the twenty Africans at Jamestown, the *Rainbowe* sailed for Madeira with a cargo of saltfish and staves. Returning, the vessel touched the Guinea Coast in search of the easy money the slavers were making. At the point of its landing, however, the *Rainbowe* found some London vessels already waiting. But very few slaves were for sale at the moment, so the Yankees and the Londoners decided on a little horseplay to brighten a dull Sunday afternoon. Pretending that a quarrel existed between the ships and the natives on shore, crew members fired a volley from their small cannon at a peaceful-looking little village, killed many of the inhabitants, and captured others. When the smoke cleared away and the prank was over, the vessels divided the slaves among them. The Boston ship received just two as its share.

Slave Ships

O N THE high seas the African captives suffered new
horrors. Herded together on deck, they were immediately handcuffed to one another and chains were
riveted to their legs. Between decks, in the space which
they were to occupy for the next two months, they were
packed spoon-fashion. There was not room to stand,
often not enough to sit. In these dark and filthy holds,
lying week after week in the same positions, without
sunlight or sanitation, with no decent food and not
enough water, with little or no exercise, their bodies de-

veloped painful sores. Kicked when they whimpered, flogged when they fainted or complained, the dazed and bewildered Africans naturally became the victims of diseases which thrive under these conditions.

One of these diseases frightened even the most hardened slavers when it appeared. Called ophthalmia, it was like the wrath of an angry God on these guilty ships. When it struck, it spared neither man nor child, neither bound nor free. The captain and his crew were as likely to become infected as were the people in chains. For that reason there was panic aboard whenever a slave began having trouble with his eyes.

Some captains took to throwing overboard any captive who showed the first symptom. They considered this a reasonable measure, since otherwise they stood to lose the whole cargo. Total blindness was the final result of the plague, and what good was a blind slave? What good was a blind crew member or captain, for that matter? But this method of fighting ophthalmia didn't always work. Often the disease continued to spread in spite of the terrible preventive.

Never was the horror of ophthalmia seen more vividly than in the case of the French slaver *Le Rodeur*, which sailed from Africa with one hundred and sixty slaves in 1819. Because his slaves showed a spirit of revolt in the early part of the voyage, the captain of *Le Rodeur* ordered all of them confined to the lower hold for the rest of the trip, without even the short daily exercise period above deck which was sometimes allowed. When oph-

thalmia hit the ship, it spread rapidly and perhaps unnoticed as a result of this complete confinement.

The first measure taken by the slaver was to isolate
the sufferers. Instead of curing the sick ones, however,
his efforts resulted only in the spread of the disease.
Soon, every captive aboard was infected. Then, one by
one, the crew members had trouble with their eyes.
Finally the ship's surgeon and the captain went blind.
The vessel sailed in darkness. There wasn't a useful pair
of eyes aboard.

With no one to steer the ship, they drifted for many
days and daily expected the vessel to crash beneath them
on some strange and rocky shore. The danger seemed
especially near when they ran into a storm so violent that
it shook and strained the ship almost to a breaking point.
But after many hours of tossing, the waves subsided and
Le Rodeur drifted into a calm. Then it was that a sound
of splashing nearby convinced those on board *Le Rodeur*
that they had drifted alongside another vessel.

A cry arose in the ship. Every man on deck shouted
anxiously. A moment later a similar outburst came from
the men on hammocks below, and this was followed by
cries from the captives chained in the hold. Almost immediately an answer came from the other ship, and a
panic of excitement followed on *Le Rodeur*. When he
was able to silence his jabbering, half-delirious crew, the
blind captain made his way to a deck rail and cupped
his hands.

"Ship ahoy! Ahoy! What ship?" he cried.

The answer came distinctly. "We're the *Saint Leon* of Spain. Help us, for God's sake!"

"We need help ourselves," said the captain of *Le Rodeur*.

"But we're dying," said the voice from the *Saint Leon*. "We're dying of hunger and thirst. Set your own price, but send someone on board to help us."

"We can give you food but not hands," *Le Rodeur's* captain replied. "Come on board and we'll exchange provisions with you for men."

"We'll pay you in money," said the Spaniard. "We'll pay you double. We'll pay a thousandfold."

"But we can't send men," the Frenchman answered. "We have slaves aboard. They've infected us with ophthalmia. We're all stone blind."

The *Saint Leon* didn't answer at once, but suddenly a fit of laughter broke out on her deck, and the helpless, blind captain of *Le Rodeur* shouted angrily, "What's the matter, man? Are you crazy?"

"No, it's not that," the hysterical voice said. "It's just that we're blind too."

The *Saint Leon* drifted away and was not heard of again. *Le Rodeur* had better luck. One man of her crew recovered his sight enough to guide the vessel into the port of Guadaloupe, an island of the West Indies. But the ship's surgeon and eleven others remained permanently blind. The captain and four men regained the use of one eye, and only five members of the crew fully recovered sight. Of the slaves, thirty-nine never saw daylight again. The rest recovered partial vision and lived on in a kind of dim twilight.

Not all slave ships suffered horrors equal to the experience of *Le Rodeur*. On the other hand, not all fared as well. One thing is definite. All the crossings were grim ordeals. Only those captives who were unusually strong to begin with survived this terrible Middle Passage, as it was called. And that is why Negroes in the New World were able to survive under conditions of oppression which wiped out the Indians of the Caribbean islands and which many other people could not have endured.

The Harbor of Le Cap

THE island of Haiti, known to the Spaniards as Santo Domingo and to the French as Saint Domingue, became the first important anchorage for the slaver in the New World. Cap François, later called Cap Français and now known as Cap-Haitien, was its main harbor in those days, and into it sailed most of the vessels whose voyages made the epoch of slavery shameful. By those who anchored there and by those who lived nearby, the harbor was familiarly known as "Le Cap." Its beauty has always been a thing to dream about, but slavery gave Le Cap a strange and violent history.

During the colonial period this great slave mart became the richest overseas possession in the world. Its planters made millions and its trade supplied two-thirds of all French imports and exports. All this happened at a time when the United States was still a wilderness. The leading men of colonial Haiti visited Europe with long lines of mulatto and Negro servants. They took the most elegant suites in the best hotels and entertained like mad princes. Before long, people everywhere were calling Le Cap the Paris of the New World.

There was excellent reasons for this reputation. Le Cap was a city of paved streets, stone houses and fine squares. It had many churches, two large hospitals, a theater, a bathing house, cafés, and gambling establishments. Its dreamy creole belles—many of them mulattoes or quadroons—leaned over the wrought-iron balconies of the houses. Young Frenchmen, impressed by their beauty, called them "the sirens."

In the half-century which led up to the French Revolution, a stream of down-and-out aristocrats poured into this rich island in the hope of regaining their lost fortunes and returning to Paris to live once more in luxury in the court of the king. Before long the island was overrun by them, and a new creole nobility was born. It must not be forgotten, however, that the prosperity of this richest of all colonies rested squarely on the naked backs of black slaves. It was they who worked the huge sugar plantations. And since they were not paid wages, profits were large. From the standpoint of the planter, the aristocrat who was in a hurry to make a fortune and get back to Paris, this was certainly a fine arrangement. The slave was not so sure. Neither was the poor white, nor the free mulatto, as we shall see.

More than a million Negroes had been brought into the island of Haiti by 1750. One who tried to count them, of course, could find only about half that number. The other half-million had either committed suicide, been starved or worked to death, or lost their lives by some other means. The death rate among slaves in the island at that time was two and one-half per cent higher than the birth rate. Slaves died—or were killed—at such a rate that the Negroes would have vanished as completely as the Indians in forty years had the slave ships stopped bringing in replacements. Opponents of slavery in France pointed out that the death rate of slaves on these Haitian plantations was greater than the death rate among soldiers during a bloody battle, that it was a third higher than the death rate among hospital patients in Lyons. Every year one-ninth of the slaves in colonial Haiti died. But immediately after slavery was abolished, this situation was changed, and the population increased rapidly.

The explanation was easy. Some planters figured that it was cheaper to work a slave to death in seven years and then replace him with a new one than to try to prolong the captive's life. Other planters followed the practice of working their slaves out in four years. The methods by which this was accomplished were, of course, inhuman, but the planter had only one aim in mind; to make a quick fortune and then retire to Paris. Slaves were compelled to be in the fields long before sunrise. They were required to stay at their work till after dark with only a few moments in which to swallow their food. Three or four hours of sleep a night was all the slave was allowed.

The Black Code, a set of rules intended to govern the relationship between slave and master in the French colonies, stated the amount of food that each slave was supposed to receive daily. In the island of Haiti, however, planters were in too great a hurry to pay much attention to these rules. Not one aristocrat in five provided food for his slaves. Instead, the custom was to evade the law by marking off a tiny plot of ground and requiring the slave to raise his own food. The trouble with this plan was that the slave had no time to cultivate his garden, and the result was that hungry slaves roved the countryside at night like packs of starving wolves in search of food.

Soon, however, the problem in Haiti became more complicated. One danger that arose, from the point of view of the planter nobility, was part of the general prosperity. Black slaves came to outnumber their masters by ten to one. That was the way it had to be to keep up the level of profit. Under these conditions the drivers of slaves who had practiced cruelties and horrors began to feel a little uneasy. What if the slaves should suddenly realize their power? To make sure that would not happen, they added more cruelties.

Another complication bothered the island aristocracy even more. That was the growing numbers and influence of two other social groups in the colony. One of these was the poor whites called *petit blancs.* The other was known as the free men of color, *hommes de couleur libre.* The poor whites consisted of unsuccessful fortune hunters, stranded adventurers, scattered pirate crews, wandering portrait painters, circus performers, shop keepers, exiles and the like. The free men of color were mainly the mulatto offspring of the planter nobility and their slave mistresses.

These groups were about equal in size, but each included from two to three times as many people as made up the ruling class of planters—of whom there were about ten thousand at the time of the colony's greatest prosperity. The people in each of these social groups were held under the thumbs of the planter group at the top by very simple means; the aristocrats set one against the other. To do this they told the poor whites how fortunate they were just to be white, even though they were hungry and ignorant and mistreated. They told them that no matter how downtrodden they might be, they could always console themselves by remembering that they were white and therefore better than any man of color. To make this poor argument sound a little more convincing, the planters gave the poor whites certain po-

litical rights which they denied to the mulattoes—
though never enough to enable them to become a threat
to the real rulers of the island.

To the free men of color the planters said, in effect:
"We do not oppose you. Those poor whites are to blame."
To make this sound believable they could point to the
general prosperity of the mulatto class, for the free men
of color were well-to-do compared to the poor whites.
About one-tenth of all the plantations of the island belonged to them, and large numbers of their group had
been sent to Paris by their white fathers to be educated
and to escape the unhappy conditions on the island. At
the same time the planters were perfectly frank about
their relations with their dark mistresses and often as-
sumed normal responsibility for their mulatto children.

In this way the colonial nobility of ten thousand was
able to hold in line the thirty thousand poor whites, the
thirty thousand free men of color, and the eight hundred
thousand slaves. Naturally they were pleased with themselves. A time came, however, when wit was not a sub-
stitute for justice. A very complicated train of events led
to a complete smashup.

One of the important factors was the enlightenment
of the mulattoes educated in Paris. Among the sons born
to upper-class Frenchmen and their island mates were
a number of outstanding geniuses. The father of Alexandre Dumas, born in Haiti of a black mother, became a
general in the French army. His son, the author of *The
Three Musketeers, The Count of Monte Cristo* and

scores of other romantic novels, became one of the
world's best-loved writers. A grandson, Alexandre Dumas, fils, wrote *Camille,* the novel and play upon which
the opera *La Traviata* is based. Then there was John
James Audubon, the painter of birds who later came to
the United States. The father of this great artist took the
boy and a daughter back to France when disorders broke
out on the island. Jean Louis, offspring of still another
mixed union in colonial Haiti, became the most famous
swordsman and duellist in Napoleon's armies. Many
others, less celebrated than these perhaps, were nevertheless men of superior intelligence and courage, and a
good number were born with a bright flame of patriotism
in their hearts.

Moreover they were not without skill or training in the
art of war. While they had been denied civil rights at
home, they had not been exempted from compulsory
military service. That is why the Compte d'Estaing,
leader of the French force which fought so bravely for
the American side at the Siege of Savannah in 1779, was
able to include detachments of these Haitian mulattoes
in the army with which he engaged the British in
Georgia.

Vincent Ogé and his friend Jean Baptiste Chavannes
were young men of this group. Both loved the island on
which they were born. It was Ogé's wish to return home
from France, when his education abroad was completed,
and help the free men of color of Haiti to gain the constitutional justice which the rulers of the island had de-

nied them. His aim was to arouse his people and to take by force, if necessary, the rights to which they were entitled.

Already in France the General Assembly had passed laws granting the free mulattoes their request for fair participation in the political life of the colony, but the laws were ignored by the island government, and nothing happened. In fact, the colonial aristocrats began to talk about withdrawing from the French nation and running the island to suit themselves. There the matter hung, despite the fact that the prevailing sentiment in France, where there had just been a revolution, favored Ogé and Chavannes and the group they represented. So it was back to Haiti for this young patriot and a showdown with the colonial authorities.

On the way home he stopped first in London where he gained an interview with Thomas Clarkson, Secretary of the English Abolitionist Society. With Clarkson's help he crossed the ocean to Charleston, where he met Americans in South Carolina who were strongly opposed to slavery and who not only arranged his passage to Haiti but also provided him with money to purchase arms. Soon he was on his way again. In Haiti he was met by his own brothers as well as by Chavannes, and in due time an American sloop dropped anchor at the appointed place and put ashore muskets and ammunition enough to arm three hundred men.

Ogé and Chavannes rallied a group of followers and set out bravely, but their little company was defeated and scattered on a country road, and the eager young leaders had to flee into Santo Domingo, the Spanish half of the island. There they were captured and returned to Le Cap, where the authorities not only condemned them but put them to death publicly by the cruel method of breaking them on the wheel. The colonial aristocracy thought this would be a lesson to others who might have similar intentions. Here again their wit failed them. Ogé and Chavannes were looked upon as martyrs by the people of their own group. A spirit of rebellion grew, and before long there was serious trouble on the island.

Up to now the struggle was a three-cornered affair between aristocrats, poor whites, and free mulattoes. The droves of hungry slaves looked on without seeming to understand or care too much which way the conflict went. As they saw it, there was little to choose between aristocratic whites and well-to-do mulattoes, for both held slaves at that time. The poor whites were even worse in their sight, for many of them knuckled down to the aristocrats and consented to do the ugly work of driving and beating the slaves. Other poor whites fought the slaves for the scraps that were thrown from the kitchens of the masters.

But it was a mistake to suppose, as the upper groups did, that this meant the slaves were unaware of what was happening. Actually they watched every move. As always happens under slavery or any other form of oppression, some of those oppressed were men and women of character and intellect. A few had found ways of educating themselves secretly, and they were fully able to understand the conflict on their own island as well as what had just happened in France during the Revolution. Among those who watched and understood in Haiti was a slender black man named Toussaint, a coachman on the Bréda plantation near Le Cap, a slave soon to prove himself one of the truly great men of the Western World.

While the aristocrats maneuvered to stay in control by keeping the poor whites and the mulattoes fighting each other, the black slaves of Haiti suddenly rose up and claimed their rights as men. And Toussaint, thereafter known as L'Ouverture or the Opener, wrote a short message that caused their hearts to pound and the island to shake:

> Brothers and Friends:
> My name is perhaps known to you. I have undertaken to avenge your wrongs. It is my desire that liberty and equality shall reign. I am striving to this end. Come and unite with us, brothers, and combat with us for the same cause.
> Your very humble and obedient servant,
> TOUSSAINT L'OUVERTURE,
> *General for the Public Welfare.*

The Coachman of Bréda

HOW they responded to the call and how they fought under the leadership of the amazing Toussaint is one of history's wonders. The aroused Negroes went into battle armed with knives, picks, hoes, and sticks with iron points. They charged into bayonets without fear or care, assured that if they were killed they would wake up in Africa. They clutched at the horses of the French Dragoons and pulled the riders to the ground. They reached down into the mouths of the cannon and tried to pull out the bullets. When the charges went off, they

72

were blown to pieces, but others climbed over the guns and fell upon the gunners with bare hands. They could not be stopped.

Until he was nearly fifty years old, François Dominique Toussaint had seen nothing of soldiers or the military life. He had been a first-rate coachman on the Bréda plantation, and his thoughtful habits had been noted by a few people, but no one suspected him of genius. His highest achievement in the community up to that time was in medicine, in which he had picked up enough skill to treat the slaves of the estate. His success was such that he received calls from neighboring plantations, and some of the masters occasionally asked for him when members of their own families were stricken with tropical diseases. His manner was so kindly and his understanding of human nature so sure that those who knew him best called him *"old* Toussaint," though he was still full of vigor.

The thousand or more slaves on the Bréda plantation were treated better than most, thanks to a benevolent French owner and to the kindly manager he placed in charge of his property. In this atmosphere the "First of the Blacks," as histories now describe him, was born and grew to strong and thoughtful manhood. His swimming was excellent; his horsemanship even better. At least one person who saw him in the saddle called him the "Centaur of the Savannas."

Toussaint's father was a free black laborer employed on the same plantation. He had been owned by the Jesuit

Fathers when they kept a school in Le Cap, and from them he had learned to read and write and to quote passages from the classics. When this order was banished from the colony, the Fathers liberated their slaves, and the parent of Toussaint was among those given freedom. He married a slave woman, however, and his children remained in bondage. But this did not prevent him from teaching his meditative son the things that he himself had learned in books. And when friends of the blacks arose in France and preached the worth and dignity of all men, irrespective of color or condition of servitude, no one anywhere read their words with more under-standing than did the coachman of Bréda. This para-graph from the writings of the Abbé Raynal made a special impression on him:

> Nations of Europe, your slaves will break the yoke that weighs upon them. The Negroes only lack a leader. Where is that great man to be found? He will appear, we cannot doubt it; he will show himself to raise the sacred standard of liberty and to gather around him his companions in misfortune. More impetuous than the moun-tain torrents, they will leave behind them on all sides the ineffaceable signs of their resentment. The old world as well as the new will applaud him. The name of the hero who will have re-established the rights of the human species will be blessed forever.

Toussaint's reading did not stop here, though it is plain that he considered this a statement of his own destiny. His favorite philosopher was the Greek Epictetus who himself had been a slave and whose writings Toussaint found in a French translation, and he consoled himself with such passages as the one which says:

> Man is not the master of man, but death is, and life and pleasure and pain; for if he comes without these things, bring Caesar to me and you will see how firm I am. But if I shall release myself from my masters, that is from the things by means of which masters are formidable, what further trouble have I, what master have I still?

Naturally a coachman slave who had spent twenty years brooding on such matters could not be wholly unprepared when the clash came. The same could not be said for most of those he sought to free. They were the hungry host hanging on the edge of starvation, unable to contemplate anything but the pains in their stomachs. They knew nothing about military organization. Few slaves knew how to load or fire a gun. None had access to arms when the trouble broke.

With this kind of human material Toussaint L'Ouverture challenged the most powerful armies Europe could send abroad, including some trained by Napoleon Bonaparte himself. With such forces as he was able to gather from the slave quarters of Haiti he met, defeated, and sometimes annihilated forces more powerful than any that participated in the American Revolution. He made wonderful soldiers of men who previously had been trembling slaves, and he commanded disciplined armies larger than any George Washington ever saw.

The career of Toussaint as soldier, patriot, and statesman began by torchlight in a Haitian glade with an uprising of slaves in 1791. It ended in the gray dampness
of the medieval prison at Fort de Joux near the Swiss
frontier of France in 1803. In this short span of years he
saw, over and over again, the miracle of hungry, suicidal
slaves transformed into men of strength, courage, and
sometimes heroism. He saw a rabble moulded into
marching battalions and cavalry divisions. And he saw
these legions, which he himself had organized, hurl back
the French, the British, and the Spanish in turn. Finally,
he saw slavery abolished in the French nation and the
complete independence of Haiti assured.

He was captured treacherously in the end by representatives of Napoleon who had met to negotiate with
him, and he was removed to the prison in the Alps where
he finally died in misery. Toussaint's father reached the
age of one hundred and six and might have lived longer
had he not been put to death by the French in Haiti. It
seems likely too that Toussaint could have served his
country many more years had it not been for his harsh
imprisonment. However, even his death was a sort of
victory for mankind in its long and patient struggle for
freedom, for Toussaint was eulogized by some of
France's greatest writers, and his passing inspired William Wordsworth to write a sonnet that is still alive and
full of meaning:

> Toussaint, the most unhappy Man of Men!
> Whether the rural Milk-maid by her Cow

Sing in thy hearing, or thou liest now
Alone in some deep dungeon's earless den,
O miserable chieftain! where and when
Wilt thou find patience? Yet die not; do thou
Wear rather in thy bonds a cheerful brow:
Though fallen Thyself, never to rise again,
Live, and take comfort. Thou hast left behind
Powers that will work for thee; air, earth, and skies;
There's not a breathing of the common wind
That will forget thee; thou hast great allies;
Thy friends are exultations, agonies,
And love, and Man's unconquerable mind.

Eighth Wonder of the World

I T WOULD be a mistake to think that the victories of
the Haitians under Toussaint were all won by swarm-
ing over the enemy and overpowering him with numbers.
The campaigns and strategy which brought them success have been recorded with much detail. They fill
many books and reveal indisputably that the genius of
Toussaint L'Ouverture in war and in statesmanship was
fully as important to total victory in the island as the
blood and sweat of the former slaves.

Among the tactics used by them was one which aimed

to exhaust the invader. When they were unable to meet the enemy in a pitch battle, due to lack of weapons or shortage of ammunition, the Haitians withdrew to the hills. At night they would return in small detachments and commence beating drums, firing rifles, and shouting at the top of their lungs. Then they would slip away quietly again as the enemy rose up and charged into the darkness. The next night the same thing was repeated. Never knowing which of these feints would turn into a bloody attack, the enemy had to take them all seriously. In time, sleepless nights and startled awakenings wore the soldiers down. They were unable to fight effectively, and they became easy victims of tropical diseases.

It took this and more to turn back the armies that were thrown at the Haitians. Napoleon had come to power in France, and one of his ambitions was to set up an overseas empire in the Western Hemisphere. The first step was to establish his power in Haiti. He wanted to start by stepping on Toussaint as a man would step on a cockroach, but two things restrained him. First, he was already engaged in hostilities with Great Britain. Second, visitors from Haiti, among them, no doubt, veterans who had crossed swords with the black general, advised him not to underestimate the forces he would have to meet on the island. Napoleon took both into consideration.

But as soon as his hands were free in Europe, he started working on plans. First he tried to flatter Toussaint into bringing the island back under French rule. When this failed, he sent representatives to talk more firmly. Toussaint stood his ground so stubbornly and yet answered so politely that Napoleon went into a rage. He banished the commissioner who had brought the messages and began making preparations for a mighty expedition against Haiti.

In the ports of France, Spain, and Holland hundreds of ships were assembled. They were distributed in many harbors so that no one would know just how large an invasion he meant to send. Soldiers of France were ordered to march to all these ports of embarkation. Among them were regiments which had seen action in Germany, Italy and Egypt; some of the best units in Europe. In two years France sent forty thousand of her finest into this campaign. At the head of the expedition Napoleon placed General Le Clerc, one of France's great generals who also happened to be his own brother-in-law, the husband of Napoleon's sister Pauline. Eventually, Napoleon hoped, a Bonaparte would sit on a rich island throne in the Caribbean.

This was the expedition that Toussaint and his soldiers met. The campaign lasted many months, with both sides suffering hardships and losses. For a long time it seemed that the armies of Le Clerc would surely win, but this was followed by a period in which the outcome appeared doubtful. Then the tide turned completely. It now became plain that the invaders could *not* win. The Haitians under Toussaint were growing stronger and stronger as the veterans of Napoleon's triumphs weakened. Victory was already in sight when the French trapped and captured Toussaint by pretending to negotiate with him under a flag of truce.

Moreover, there were other strong men ready to take up the fight and complete the liberation of the island. Among these were two whose genius in war, if not in all other matters, was scarcely less than that of Toussaint himself. Jean Jacques Dessalines, a sullen and angry man, a former slave with the marks of many beatings on his back, a black man whose hatred of all whites had grown so bitter he would not look one in the face, took command. When Dessalines finally put down his sword, the French could count sixty thousand graves in Haiti. It was Napoleon's most costly effort up to that time, and the result was total defeat. Dessalines had himself crowned emperor with the title of Jacques I.

When the fury of war subsided, however, this man who couldn't forget the marks on his back was unprepared for the responsibilities that fall on a peacetime leader of a nation. Things were soon in such a muddle that his own men assassinated him. Henri Christophe, the third hero of Haiti's independence, then rose to power.

Christophe is believed to have been with the Haitians at the Siege of Savannah, perhaps as an officer's servant, for he was only a boy at the time. Later he had worked in a hotel of Le Cap. Either at Savannah, where white men and brown and black fought side by side for liberty and justice in the American colony of Georgia, or in the *Hôtel de la Couronne*, where the visitors from Europe were as likely to be courageous friends of the blacks as they were to be slavers, he had learned that there is a Cause that makes men brothers. He never seemed to believe, as did Dessalines, that being black or brown or white was in any sense a measure of one's worth.

Mainly Christophe occupied himself with the creation of a court and the building of palaces and a great fortress. Perhaps his years in the *Couronne* had taught him to admire the elegant manners of the elite. He set up a nobility of princes, dukes, counts, and barons, following the pattern of European monarchies. There was nothing comic about it, however. The former hotel waiter knew a great deal about quality. His own crown, scepter, and mace, made by the jewelers of Le Cap, are masterpieces of the goldsmith's art. He built a church just for his coronation and had it torn down afterwards.

That was only the beginning. A skilled brick mason himself, Christophe delighted in construction. He had twelve palaces built for himself in various parts of his realm. The greatest of these was Sans Souci, and its majestic ruin still stands at Milot, about fourteen miles from Cap-Haitien. To see the ruin today is to realize that, when it was built, Christophe's palace was fully as impressive as the finest French chateaux.

The palace of Sans Souci was an astonishing achievement. But the Citadel Christophe erected on the summit of La Ferriere, a mountain overlooking Milot and the harbor of Le Cap, is awe-inspiring. Historians still speak of the Seven Wonders of the Ancient World, including the Pyramids of Egypt, the Hanging Gardens of Babylon, the Statue of Zeus, the Temple of Diana at Ephesus, the Mausoleum of Halicarnassus, the Colossus at Rhodes, and the Pharos (a lighthouse) at Alexandria, but some who have seen Christophe's Citadel feel justified in calling it the World's eighth wonder. Gérman Arciniegas, the South American writer, goes even further. He names it "the first wonder of liberty."

No descriptions do justice to the Citadel, though some books devote many chapters to it. People still wonder how the black king got the heavy cannon up the mountain sides to their present positions. It is hard enough for an ordinary person to make the trip by mule-back, carrying nothing. Christophe distrusted the enemies who had so treacherously taken Toussaint, and he meant his Citadel to be both fortress and refuge should Haitian liberty be threatened again. He planned it on a scale that would allow fifteen thousand men to resist siege for a whole year behind its walls. In it were stored enough arms to supply such an army. While Christophe lived, he also kept it stocked with food and medicine as a precaution against a sudden attack. The perishable things were changed every three months.

Three hundred cannon guarded the great fortress, peeping out of high openings in a wall four feet thick at its base. Inside was every kind of small weapon. The army knew exactly what to do in case of another invasion. So did the people of the cities and villages of northern Haiti. Their plan of defense was to burn every house, barn, and bridge and flee to the hills. The enemy would thus be left without a shelter.

The Citadel was never used. Haiti's troubles in the years that followed were of another kind. Soon the island's government was divided into two parts, with Christophe ruling in the North and Alexandre Pétion, a man more suited to the problems of peace, in the South. Pétion belonged to the free mulatto group as represented by Ogé and Chavannes. He was a statesman of training and refinement, and it is to him, more perhaps than to anyone else, that Haitians credit their constitutional democracy.

Citizens of Venezuela honor Pétion for a different reason. When Simon Bolivar's fortunes were at low ebb, Pétion received the South American emancipator hospitably. In Haiti, to which Pétion's sympathetic friendship had drawn him, Bolivar planned the campaign which led to Venezuela's independence. Pétion supplied both men and money for the expedition. When asked by Bolivar what he wanted in return, Pétion made only one demand. He required that the slaves be set free in the territory liberated by Bolivar's arms. This was agreed, and the promise was honored by Bolivar. Consequently, a monument to Pétion stands today in the city of Caracas.

The Bondage

New People

COLONIAL HAITI was more than a western anchorage for British, Spanish and French slavers.
In another sense it was the hub of a wheel—a wheel
whose spokes reached out from Le Cap to Barbados and
Trinidad in one direction, to the Guianas and Central
America in another, to Jamaica and Mexico in another,
and to Cuba and the United States in still another. In all
of these directions there was trading in slaves, and the
number of African captives increased rapidly throughout the New World. In the West Indies and in parts of

South and Central America, the Negroes greatly out-
numbered the European colonists.

Present-day census figures for the countries of Latin
America and the Caribbean region do not always reveal
the African origin of their people. Argentina, for example, received many slaves, and the Negro population
of her capital city was large as late as 1850, but all of
these have now been absorbed, and Argentina is thought
of as a country without Negroes. The same is true of
Uruguay. In all the colonies settled by Spain, France,
and Portugal the melting pot included many Negroes.

In countries like Brazil and Venezuela and Mexico, the
dark mixture blended Indian as well as African with the
European strain. A new people has resulted, a people
which is no closer to one of these backgrounds than to
the other, but a product of all three, a new creation in a
new world.

In the United States, too, slavery produced a new
people, though not entirely in the same way. Anglo-
Saxon attitudes, based mainly on the way the Protestant
mind dealt with the problem of slavery, opposed the
mixing of people in this way. In practice this did not
necessarily mean that fewer mulatto children were born
to slave mothers in the United States than in Latin
America. It meant more often that the mulatto child of
a slave woman was surer to remain a slave and to be considered a Negro here than in the other countries. It
meant that no amount of mixing would ever cause a person who had a single Negro ancestor, no matter how far

back, to be counted as anything but a Negro unless he decided to keep his background a secret. So the color of one's ancestors became something like a mark of caste in the United States.

But the Negroes who lived under the mark also became a new people in actual fact. First there was a blending among them of all the tribes of Africa from which slaves were taken, and that in itself was most important. Even if extensive mixing with Indian neighbors and with white masters had not followed upon their arrival on these shores, the mixing of so many different African elements would have produced a people never before known on earth.

All of this happened, however, and all of it must be remembered if one is to know the people who came to make up one-tenth of the American nation or to understand their story.

Meanwhile in South America, along the march of the Spanish conquistadors, the mingling of newcomers from Europe and Africa produced a saint—or a man who may yet become one. He was Martín de Porres, the son of a free Negro woman of Panama and a Castilian nobleman. Born in the old city of Lima, Peru, December 8, 1579, Martín was baptized in the Church of San Sebastian on the same day. The register was properly signed by Antonio Polanco, a priest now famous for having also baptized St. Rose of Lima, the first canonized saint of the Americas.

One of the things that marked the childhood of Martín
was his tender understanding of small creatures. The
same fondness, the same understanding and sympathy
marked his dealings with the sick and destitute people
who needed him after he became a Dominican Brother.
Miracles of generosity and healing flowed from his hands
as he went through the streets of Lima and, after he died,
pilgrims came from great distances to pray at his shrine
for the same benefits.

Many beautiful legends are now associated with the
story of the Blessed Martín. All of them emphasize the
worthiness and charity of a man who was not only devoted to the ministry of the church but was a physician
and a pioneer social worker besides. Today there are
orphanages and hospitals, as well as churches and altars,
to commemorate him.

America's Crispus Attucks

IT WAS forty-three years after the landing of the first
Negro captives before Virginia passed an act which
made the bondage or freedom of a child hereditary, de-
pending on the status of the mother. It was not till 1705
that the laws of Virginia permitted a man of property to
list people in his inventory as real estate. So all together
it took nearly a century for the condition of the Africans
at Jamestown to degenerate into actual slavery.

And right along with slavery came the opposition to
slavery. Just twenty-six years after Virginia established

slavery as hereditary, a protest was made in German-town, Pennsylvania, against the barter of human flesh within the borders of the colonies. This was the first formal action of its kind, but sentiment against the system was expressed in many places. Attitudes of disapproval thrived best, of course, in sections where the farming did not lend itself so well to slave labor.

People who profited by slavery were inclined to close their eyes to its evil side. Those to whom it was unprofitable were more ready to examine it from a moral point of view. In time, a rivalry grew up between the industrial part of the country where slavery was of little value and the plantation section which could not get along so well without it. Even before the American Revolution the northern colonies were showing more interest than those of the South in plans to abolish slavery.

The first antislavery society in America was founded through Quaker influence with Benjamin Franklin as its president. John Adams, Thomas Jefferson, Patrick Henry, and George Washington all expressed strong wishes to see the practice ended, sooner or later, in the United States. But most plantation owners had other ideas, as Washington pointed out in a letter to Lafayette. To this hero, who aided the American cause so nobly during the Revolutionary War and who was himself a member of the French abolitionist society known as Friends of the Blacks, Washington wrote that, while petitions for the abolition of slavery had been presented to the Virginia legislature, they had little chance of being considered.

In England, too, great friends of mankind opposed slavery. John Wesley preached against it. Samuel Johnson, Adam Smith, Edmund Burke, Charles Fox, and the younger William Pitt all stressed the economic or moral wrong of the system. Thomas Clarkson and William Wilberforce fought valiantly for its abolishment and with their friends and supporters won the fight in Britain and eventually in the dominions.

This struggle for the freedom of the slaves was pushed into the background by the trouble which began between the American colonies and England. Bad feeling between the mother country and the colony had been increasing for about ten years, but the first clash of Americans with British soldiers took place on the 5th of March, 1770, and this incident was important for two reasons. First, as Daniel Webster said, it marked the break of the colonies away from the British Empire. Second, it was in this clash that the first man to die in the War for American freedom fell. He happened to be a Negro.

His name was Crispus Attucks, and most of what we know about his earlier life comes from a notice found in *The Boston Gazette,* or *Weekly Journal* of October 2, 1750, twenty years before he gave his life for his country. It says:

> "Ran away from his master WILLIAM BROWN of Farmingham, on the 30th of Sept. last, a Mulatto Fellow, about 27 years of Age, named CRISPUS, 6 Feet 2 Inches high, short curl'd Hair, his

Knees nearer together than common; had on a
light colour'd Bear-skin Coat, plain brown Fus-
tain Jacket, or brown all-wool one, new Buckskin
Breeches, blue Yarn Stockings, and a checked
woolen Shirt.

"Whoever shall take up said Runaway, and
convey him to his above-said Master, shall have
ten Pounds, old Tenor Reward, and all necessary
Charges paid. And all Masters of Vessels and
others, are hereby cautioned against concealing
or carrying off said Servant on Penalty of the
Law."

This advertisement was run again on the 13th and the
20th of the following month, which showed that the tall,
slightly knock-kneed fellow in the blue yarn stockings
and the checkered woolen shirt had not been found. In
fact, whether or not he was ever returned to his owner
is a matter that was not recorded, but his name did appear again in the newspapers of Boston. It also appeared
many years later engraved on a monument on Boston
Common.

Seven British soldiers came up State Street with
pointed bayonets on that night of March 5th, clearing
everything before them. A group of Americans, forty or
fifty in number, waited near the head of the street in the
heart of the city. They were led by this same Attucks,
more recently employed on a whaling vessel. Their
weapons were clubs and stones. As the soldiers drew
near, Attucks shouted, "The way to get rid of these soldiers is to attack the main guard."

At this signal the Americans filled the air with rocks

and sticks. The red coats opened fire. The tall mulatto in the foreground was an easy target. He was the first to fall. The second shot killed Samuel Gray as he stepped toward the fallen Attucks. James Caldwell, a sailor, and Samuel Maverick, a boy of seventeen, were both wounded so severely they died later.

Attucks and Caldwell, both men of the sea, were carried to Faneuil Hall. The bodies of the others were removed to their homes. Bells rang. People ran out into the streets. Later a huge crowd went to Faneuil Hall to see the faces of the dead heroes. After the funeral, a procession six columns deep followed the four hearses, and all four men were buried in one grave.

Despite the patriotic example of Crispus Attucks, however, the American colonies were slow to accept Negroes into the army. Perhaps they wondered about holding a man in slavery after he had risked his life for his country. But in 1775 the British governor of Virginia offered freedom to all slaves who would join the King's army in its fight against the American revolutionists, and this forced the colonies to change their minds. They quickly realized what it would mean to their cause if the British were able to enlist large numbers of Negro slaves, and it was to offset this move by Lord Dunmore that Massachusetts, Connecticut, Rhode Island, New York, Pennsylvania, Maryland, Virginia and North Carolina arranged to accept military services from slaves. Arrangements were made whereby owners would receive payment for the slaves from the public treasury.

About three thousand Negroes took advantage of this opportunity, and more might have served if another plan had been successful. This was a proposal to organize an army of Negroes in the South by paying slave owners one thousand dollars each for able men and then rewarding the Negro soldiers themselves by giving each his freedom, plus fifty dollars, at the end of the war. Colonel John Laurens of the Continental forces was the officer selected to recruit and organize the army, but Georgia and South Carolina refused to cooperate with Colonel Laurens, and he was unable to carry out his assignment.

There were Negro soldiers at Valley Forge, and there were others in most of the important battles of the American Revolution. At least two of these recent slaves performed acts that were singled out by the historians of the period. One occurred at the Battle of Bunker Hill when Negro Peter Salem charged forward and fired the shot that killed the boastful Major John Pitcairn of the British army. The other happened at Newport, Rhode Island, while the royal forces were there. The American Colonel, William Barton, undertook to capture the British General, Richard Prescott. His assistant on this mission was a Negro, named Prince, who actually made the capture, taking General Prescott while he was in bed.

After the war was over, New York and Rhode Island and Virginia rewarded their slave soldiers with freedom, but in general the condition of slavery remained the same for most Negro Americans.

Phillis Wheatley's America

WHILE Crispus Attucks was working on a whaling vessel, and while he was dying on Boston Common, Negro Americans elsewhere were serving their country in other ways.

On Long Island, for example, a faithful and gentle servant named Jupiter Hammon wrote poetry. In 1761 he composed and published as a broadside in New York a poem which he called "An Evening Thought. Salvation by Christ with Penetential Cries." This was the first literary work by a Negro to be printed in the United

States. Soon, however, a more important poet than Hammon came out of American slavery.

She was Phillis Wheatley, born in Senegal on the west coast of Africa, perhaps in 1753. Captured and brought to America on a slave ship in 1761, she became the personal servant of Mrs. Susannah Wheatley, wife of a Boston tailor, John Wheatley. As often happened with household slaves, where servant and master came to know each other as human beings, a warm friendship grew between the two parties, and Phillis became like one of the family. Mary Wheatley, the daughter of Mrs. Susannah, helped the dark child to learn to read, and within a few years Phillis was composing verses that charmed and astonished everyone who read them.

The Wheatleys were not the kind of people who would or could hold a sensitive young artist like Phillis in bondage, and they wasted no time arranging for her freedom. Still the delicate African girl remained with the people who had befriended her, and in 1773 she went to England in the care of Nathaniel Wheatley, the son of the family. Phillis's health was not too good in those days and a doctor had advised the Wheatleys that a sea voyage might help her.

Phillis was a success in London. At seventeen, this girl whose childhood had been marred by the horrors of a slave ship was writing poems that reminded people of the poems of Alexander Pope. Now at twenty, by her wit and grace and by her modest ways, she won many friends abroad. Among them were the Countess of Huntingdon and the Lord Mayor of London. An elegant folio copy of *Paradise Lost,* given by Brook Watson, the Lord Mayor, was one of many presents bestowed on her by Londoners.

But more important than presents and noble patronage was the publication in England of her book, *Poems on Various Subjects.* This little collection was later brought out in the United States and frequently reprinted, especially during the antislavery campaign. Between 1834 and 1838 the slender volume was issued in at least three different editions. Selections from it appeared now and again in school readers, and the example and achievement of Phillis caused many Americans to think seriously about the evil of slavery.

Phillis wrote other poems and planned another book, but it was never completed. A letter from Boston brought the word that Mrs. Susannah Wheatley was ill, so Phillis returned home from London to the bedside of her great friend. Mrs. Wheatley died a few months later. Four years afterwards, in 1778, both Mr. Wheatley and Mary, the daughter, who had helped Phillis learn to read, also died. Nathaniel was still living abroad, and with all the other Wheatleys gone, Phillis became lonely and despondent.

Then she met John Peters. Perhaps she imagined that he would bring back the sunshine. But John Peters brought her only hardship. Marriage and parenthood failed to give the merry Mr. Peters a sense of responsibility. In time Phillis had to take work in a cheap boarding house in order to support her family. Her health broke, and she died on December 5, 1784 at the age of thirty-one.

Meanwhile a middle-aged, unmarried man was working on his farm near Ellicott City in Maryland. His name was Benjamin Banneker, and one acquaintance describes him as a "large" person of "noble appearance, with venerable hair, wearing a coat of superfine drab broadcloth." Another individual got the impression that he was "of black complexion, medium stature, of uncommonly soft and gentlemanly manners and pleasing colloquial powers." But whether he was large or medium-sized, Banneker was in every other way a remarkable man for his time.

Born November 9, 1731, of free parents, he received a smattering of education at the country school near the family home in Maryland, and the first indication he gave of exceptional ability was when he made a clock by himself—a clock that kept time and struck the hours. After that nobody doubted that young Banneker was clever with his hands, but still nothing much happened. Perhaps he was too fond of liquor.

When he was twenty-seven, his father died, and Benjamin took over the running of the farm, but it was not till he was past forty that he began to show the real power of his intellect. The first revelation came when some Quakers who were building flour mills at Ellicott City came to buy provisions for their workmen at his

farm. In their friendly talks with the farmer these construction men were impressed by his interest in mathematics, and George Ellicott loaned him some books,
surveying instruments, and other materials. The books
fascinated Banneker. He seemed to get a new vision,
and in a short time he overcame the drinking habit. More
than that, he mastered the material in the books so completely that he was able to point out errors in them.

By 1789 his abilities were so well recognized that he
was asked to join the group commissioned to survey the
Federal Territory and lay out the city of Washington,
D. C. Two years later he started a series of almanacs
which were issued from year to year thereafter and
which attracted much attention both in the United
States and abroad. Banneker became, even more than
Phillis Wheatley, an example of what Negroes could
contribute to American life when given an opportunity.
His career became another strong argument against
slavery.

Unlike Phillis Wheatley, Banneker was a native-born
American. His parents, too, were native-born, though his
grandfather was an African named Banaky who was said
to have been a prince in his tribe. One of his grand-
mothers was Molly Welsh, an English woman who
started life in America as an indentured servant. After
completing her own seven years of bondage, she bought
Banaky, liberated and later married him.

Several other Negroes gained prominence in the time
of the American Revolution. Two of them were hearty

adventurers and men of the sea, one was a dapper little quadroon preacher who came to Boston from Barbados, and one was the first Negro to be educated at Princeton. The fifth was a respected physician of New Orleans. But there was one thing they had in common. All of them hated slavery. They were not men who could feel secure in their own freedom while slavery existed all around them.

With Gustavus Vassa this was easily understandable, for he was born in Benin in the region of the advanced African civilizations of the middle ages. When he was eleven years old, he was kidnapped and thrown into a slave ship bound for America. Here he was sold, first to a Virginia planter and then to a British naval officer. This second man helped him to get an education, but the Philadelphia merchant into whose hands he passed next was even more considerate. He made it possible for Vassa to purchase his freedom.

There followed a period at sea in which Vassa worked his way up to become ship's steward and saw something of the world. He finally retired from the sea to devote all of his time to work for the suppression of the slave trade. He also became associated with people in England who were sympathetic to the French Revolution. Slavery, oppression, tyranny—all of these things, he saw, were related. Under one name or flag they were as bad as under another. Gustavus Vassa is remembered mainly today because his memoirs, *The Interesting Narrative of the Life of Oloudah Equiano, or Gustavus Vassa,* helped to make it plain that the cause of the slave in the United States was a part of the world problem of oppression. It helped to put Negro Americans in touch with liberals abroad, especially in England.

Paul Cuffe's adventures were of another sort. Though he was a free-born American, the son of an African father who had purchased his own freedom and of an Indian mother, Cuffe's interest in the cause of the Negro was even greater than his passion for navigation. Born on one of the Elizabeth Islands near New Bedford, Massachusetts, he went to sea on whaling vessels when he was sixteen. By the time he was twenty, he was in business for himself, with his own boat.

His first experiences as an independent operator were not happy, and one of his worst misfortunes was the capture of his goods by pirates. But he was not discouraged, and soon thereafter he acquired a first-rate schooner. Eventually he added two brigs and several smaller vessels to his fleet. In addition to these he was able to purchase a good bit of property on land. His ships not only put into American and Caribbean ports but also sailed to Africa and Europe.

As soon as Cuffe began to acquire property and to pay taxes, he raised the question of political rights for free Negroes, and it was mainly through his efforts that Massachusetts extended the right to vote to his group as early as 1783. Cuffe used his own money to build a school in his community, even though he was unable to get other neighbors to join him in the project, and he transported settlers to Africa at his own expense. Despite many generosities of this kind, he left a substantial estate when he died. Also, he left a reputation in New Bedford that may have been partly responsible for the favorable attitude of that city toward freed men and fugitives from slavery during the abolitionist campaign.

Prince Hall was unlike Vassa and Cuffe in appearance and in background, for his father was an Englishman and his mother a mulatto woman of Barbados in the West Indies. At seventeen this small, fine-featured boy left his home on the island and worked his way to Boston on a boat. He was deeply moved by the want and suffering of the Negroes who lived there. Prince Hall took up their cause and decided to devote his life to the improvement of their lot. He became a Methodist minister and always stood strongly against injustice.

Eventually he came to the conclusion that the key to the problems of these people was to be found in co-operation. They needed to learn to work together toward common objectives. This was in Prince Hall's mind when he founded the "African Lodge, No. 459," the first organization of Masons among Negro Americans. Masonic bodies of America refused to recognize the new group, but Hall and fourteen of his associates were initiated into a lodge of the British army, then stationed near Boston.

Meanwhile, down in Oxford County, North Carolina, two prominent white gentlemen disagreed pleasantly and laid down a wager to settle the point of difference. One was convinced that Negroes were not capable of higher education. The other was firm in his opinion that with other things being equal a colored boy would do as well in college as a white one. People of the community gathered around and became interested in the debate.

The solution agreed upon was that John Chavis, known in the county as an intelligent young fellow, would be sent to Princeton as a test case. A local preacher who had recently graduated from that institution was asked to make the arrangements. Donations were raised to pay the expenses.

There is a strong tradition that John Chavis attended Princeton during the presidency of Dr. John Wither-spoon, though he may have been taught privately by this clergyman rather than enrolled as a regular student. In any case, he returned to North Carolina with an excellent education, and no doubt the Judge who bet on him collected the winnings, but the later career of this young Negro in Raleigh was even more remarkable, considering the time and place. In the slave state in which he was born Chavis conducted a preparatory school for the sons of the same men who had wondered whether or not a Negro boy could learn from books.

His school for white boys was highly regarded, and his graduates became leaders in the state in the next generation—doctors, lawyers, justices, and at least one governor of North Carolina, Charles Manley, Jr. Of his work as an educator a prominent man of the South said, "Of all the many schools maintained for the training of our youth, his was the best in the state."

Where James Derham followed his career, life was different. In his day, French and Spanish influences still prevailed in New Orleans, and sentiment toward slavery and the Negro was more like that found in Latin American countries than in the English colonies. So Derham, a man of quiet dignity, admired by the outstanding physicians of his day, practiced medicine with much success in a city that has always had its special health problems. He carried on his work without complications based on caste attitudes, established a home, joined the Episcopal Church, and apparently lived a happy life.

He had been born a slave in Philadelphia. His master, who was a physician, taught James to read and write and to assist in compounding medicines. In this, as in other medical work, the boy showed such aptitude that, when the master died, he was bought by a surgeon of the Sixteenth British Regiment stationed in Philadelphia. After the war this officer in turn sold him to Dr. Robert Dove, a physician of New Orleans. Dr. Dove not only took full advantage of Derham's ability by making him an assistant, but offered the young slave doctor the opportunity to gain his freedom on easy terms. Derham appears to have repaid the doctor's investment within two or three years, for at the end of that time he set up his own practice.

In the cosmopolitan city of New Orleans where many languages and dialects could be heard on the streets, Derham learned French and Spanish. He prospered from the start. An article about his success appeared in an

American magazine as early as 1789. European visitors to New Orleans were favorably impressed, and mentioned his work in travel books describing American life. Henri Gregoire, the French abolitionist, included Derham with Phillis Wheatley and others in a book devoted to the achievements of outstanding Negroes of the world in science, literature, and the arts up to the end of the eighteenth century.

These were the outstanding Negroes in Phillis Wheatley's America, in the America of George Washington, Thomas Jefferson, and the Revolutionary War. Washington met Phillis on one occasion and praised her verses. Jefferson didn't share his enthusiasm for Phillis Wheatley's poetry, but he was impressed by the ability of Banneker. On one point, however, there could be no difference of opinion, even in the time of Washington and Jefferson: Negroes were definitely a part of the new nation. They contributed their labor and their talents to it from the very beginning.

Freedom Is a Powerful Word

WHAT every slave wanted, of course, was freedom. Even those philosophers who tried to defend the right of men to hold other men in bondage had to admit that if you justify the master's right to enslave, you must also justify the right of the slave to try to get away. If you argue that a master may punish a slave in order to subdue him, you must grant that the slave has the right to turn on his master in an effort to win freedom.

In the days of the American Revolution the air was always full of discussion and debate in this vein. There

was also much talk about the equality of all men before
God. Slaves were not supposed to understand such matters, but they listened to their masters' conversation as
they served at table, and sometimes they bent an ear
from the driver's seat as the gentlefolk whispered in their
carriages. Without appearing to pay attention, they over-
heard talk in taverns and on the public squares. Occasionally an educated slave or free Negro gathered a
group of illiterate ones around himself in a secret place
and read from the books, papers, handbills and broad-
sides of the time. Nearly always the subject of this reading was freedom.

It was not long before the slaves themselves were convinced that they were entitled to freedom and that they
were being unjustly and sinfully held in bondage. But
what to do about it was a harder question. Some slaves
solved their problem by joining the army of the Revolution, as we have seen. Others ran away and took up with
the Indians. A few tried to reason with their masters. A
still smaller number found ways of buying their own
freedom. But all of these efforts together were small and
failed to benefit the great majority of Negroes held in
bondage.

Not until sailors began bringing reports of the successful uprising of slaves in Haiti under Toussaint L'Ouverture and his associates did large numbers of American
slaves feel encouraged to make daring attempts to win
freedom by insurrection. Many had resisted and rioted,
of course, but perhaps the first to work out a serious plan

for organized rebellion was Gabriel Prosser of Henrico County, Virginia.

This dreamy young coachman, twenty-four years old and more than six feet tall, thought it all through very carefully. He would need eleven hundred men at the start. They would meet at a brook six miles out of Richmond on the night of September 1, 1800. There they would divide into three columns, each under the command of a dependable officer, and all would march on the city at the same time. Since Richmond's population was no more than about eight thousand in those days, Gabriel was convinced that eleven hundred men could take it by moving swiftly.

The column that approached from the right would be assigned to seize the penitentiary. This building had recently been converted into an arsenal, and it contained several thousand muskets. The column on the left would be instructed to take the powder house. No weapons could be provided the men in these columns at first because there would be no way for Gabriel to get his hands on enough fire arms to go around. He did not think this a hindrance, however, for the success of their assignments would depend more on speed and surprise than on fire power. Clubs would do the job, he thought. The men could come in silently, overpower the guards in the darkness, and then take possession.

With the third column, ordered to hit the town itself, things would be different. These men were to divide themselves and enter Richmond from both ends at once.

They were to attack the general population, sparing only those believed to be friendly to their cause. Naturally, they would have to start out with arms of some sort—guns that could be secured in advance, cutlasses, knives, and pikes.

In just a few hours they would have control of Richmond. Then, with plenty of muskets and powder, with the State treasury to provide money, with the mills to give them bread, and the control of the bridge across the James River to keep off enemies from beyond, they would be solidly established, and their forces could spread out over the countryside. Within a week they would have fifty thousand men on their side, enough to enable them to attack and capture other towns.

If the plan sounds fantastic now, it didn't then. The Richmond reporter for the Boston *Chronicle* wrote immediately afterwards, "They could scarcely have failed of success, for after all, we could only muster four or five hundred men, of whom not more than thirty had muskets." But it did not succeed. A great storm arose, washing out bridges and swelling streams in Henrico County so they could not be crossed. The eleven hundred men who had answered Gabriel's call found themselves plopping around in mud up to their knees. The attack had to be postponed, and before it could be reorganized, the news leaked out, and the government took steps to protect the city and its citizens. Gabriel and a number of his associates were hunted, caught, and hanged. But a wave of fear spread over the land of slavery.

In the same year that Gabriel's rebellion failed in Virginia, Denmark Vesey, a Negro slave of Charleston, South Carolina, the personal servant of a slave-trading sea captain, bought a ticket in the East Bay-Street Lottery. He drew a prize of fifteen hundred dollars. With a part of this money he bought his freedom; with the rest he started a new life in Charleston.

He had been in bondage since he was fourteen. Now at thirty-four he went to work at the carpenter's trade, a free man. He was thrifty and energetic and got ahead. He wore a beard and made an impressive appearance. In the community in which he lived he was both admired and feared, but he was another who did not feel secure while all around him the people he knew were still in bondage. He began to plan a revolt.

Denmark Vesey was a man who respected learning. He could speak several languages, and all the men he selected to be the leaders of his rebellion were literate. They included carpenters, harness-makers, mechanics, and blacksmiths of the city. All of them were younger than Vesey, for by this time he was about fifty-six. His method was to prepare his leaders by reading to them and pointing out the arguments to be found in the Bible and in the political writings of the day which seemed to justify the slave in rising against his oppressors.

He was a convincing talker, and many slaves were ready to act when he gave the word, but one of their number informed his master, and the authorities came in swiftly and crushed the plot. Vesey and many of his associates were arrested and put to death.

Eight years later, still another startling attempt at rebellion was made by American slaves. Again the scene was Virginia, but this time the leader was a kind of plantation prophet, a man who fasted and prayed, preached and baptized, read the Bible, heard voices as he walked behind his plough, and saw visions in the sky. His name was Nat Turner.

All his life this thirty-one year old slave had believed that he was born for something special. He claimed to have seen drops of blood on the corn in the field, and, on the leaves in the woods, letters and numbers and the shapes of men. He said the spirit had told him that he must fight against the serpent but that he should first wait for the sign. When an eclipse of the sun occurred in February of 1831, Nat Turner took this for the sign that had been promised to him and rose up to prepare himself to slay his enemies with their own weapons. At this time, he later confessed, a seal was removed from his lips. That is, he became free to talk about a matter which had until then been a secret of his own heart.

Part of the reason for the seal on his lips, no doubt, was that Prophet Nat remembered how Denmark Vesey's plans had been betrayed. Perhaps the old folks of Virginia had also told him that young Gabriel failed because somebody talked. Gabriel's attempt had occurred the very year in which Nat Turner was born, and people had never stopped discussing it. Naturally, in any new plan to win freedom by rebellion the danger of betrayal had to be considered.

Nat Turner decided to confide in no one till he was ready to act. There would not be time for informing then. In the meantime, he found other ways of testing the men he expected to use and of finding out how much they wanted to be free and how far they could be trusted, and when he had singled out six on whom he could depend, he arranged a Sunday afternoon picnic in the woods, with a roasted pig and some brandy to be shared.

The barbecue lasted eleven hours, and when the group left the woods, it was after midnight, and they were ready to strike. The plan was to begin by hitting a near-by plantation, destroying the big house and its occupants, liberating the slaves and appealing to the strong ones to join the band. With the horses and weapons they hoped to capture and with the slaves they hoped to add to the attacking force, they would march on to the next plantation. By daybreak, Nat calculated, they would have strength enough to take the town of Jerusalem, the county seat.

The attacks started with a crusading fervor and at first seemed to go according to plan. The first backset occurred at a Dr. Blunt's house, where the slaves rose up and defended the master to whom they were devoted instead of joining the rebellion. This delayed the attackers and gave time for an alarm to spread. Another party was waiting to resist them when they reached the next plantation, and the band broke into small parts expecting to assemble again the following night.

But they didn't get together as planned. The militia was aroused and began to comb the countryside. Volunteer companies were sent out from Richmond, Petersburg, Norfolk, and other cities. Soon the odds against Nat Turner and his broken ranks were overwhelming. They did not meet again that night nor on any night that followed until they were reunited on the gallows.

Nat himself was the last to be captured. It took more than two months to root him out, and even then there was a gleam in his eye. His strange half-Biblical confession shows that his longing for freedom was still as strong as ever. That was a thing that wouldn't die, no matter how many rebellions were crushed or how many slaves perished.

Free Men of Color

NOT many free Negroes spent their time plotting slave revolts as did Denmark Vesey. Most of them didn't even engage in antislavery agitation as did Gustavus Vassa and Prince Hall. Many went about their work without considering the subject one way or another. A few were slaveholders who never missed a chance to defend the practice.

At the time that slavery was abolished, there were about half a million free men of color in the United States as compared to nearly four million slaves. Not all of these lived in the North; not even most of them. In New Orleans and Charleston and other southern cities there were large communities of free Negroes who became important elements in the population. This was especially true of New Orleans where about one-fifth of the city's taxable property was owned by them in 1850.

Sometimes designated on legal papers as f. m. c., *gens de couleur libre, hommes de couleur,* or h. c., these colored Americans lived during slavery about as Negroes live in the United States today. In New Orleans, the public attitude toward these people was more like that found in Cuba, Porto Rico, Martinique and the South American countries than that of the rest of the United States, and it produced an exotic social and cultural pattern in the years preceding the Civil War.

James Derham, the slave physician from Philadelphia, was only one of a long list of colored men and women of Louisiana who achieved professional and artistic success in the nineteenth century. While many had to go abroad for the opportunities they needed to make their highest marks, a number of them did surprisingly well at home. French cultural influences still predominated of course, so it was to Paris that aspiring young people went for advanced education and to find opportunities for self-expression.

In the case of the free Negro people there was a double reason for study in Europe. Social and political restrictions based on color, not unlike some of those which still exist in the South, were being felt. One of the restrictions, of course, was against intermarriage between the groups. This legislation was in delicate conflict with an old creole custom, so Louisiana men compromised by observing the letter but not the spirit of the law. White men, including some of the wealthiest and most prominent figures of New Orleans, made matches with colored girls, lived with them openly, and raised mulatto and quadroon and octoroon families. More often than not, these creole men showed genuine affection for their colored offspring, and those who could afford it sent them to Paris where, it was felt, fewer obstacles would be placed in their way.

It was from this group that most of the brightest talents came. One of the earliest to attract attention was Basil Croquere, described by the newspapers of his day as the handsomest man in New Orleans. Croquere's green broadcloth suit, his ruffles and his milk-white stock must have been something to see, but his swordsmanship was even more startling. He operated a fencing academy to which fashionable young men came to learn the art of self-defense from a past master. Nobody denied that Croquere was the best swordsman in New Orleans, which is saying a great deal when you consider that city's reputation for duelling. Basil Croquere was also interested in mathematics and philosophical problems. These interests may have been acquired in Paris, along with his graceful swordsmanship, but he brought them all back to the leafy, romantic city in which he was born.

A product of the same circles in New Orleans was Victor Séjour whose first love was poetry. In 1846 Séjour and several other colored poets put together a sheaf of the verses they had written and published them in a charming little volume called *Les Cenelles*. This book is famous now, not only because it contains the first published work by Séjour, but also because it is the first anthology of its kind by Negro Americans. Séjour went to France and became one of the most popular playwrights of Paris in the time of Alexandre Dumas and Victor Hugo.

Edmond Dédé was a musician, a violinist and composer of talent. He later became director of an orchestra in Bordeaux, France. The brothers Lucien and Sidney Lambert became concert pianists and won recognition in Europe and in South America. There were enough colored musicians in New Orleans at one time to organize a symphony orchestra. Julien Hudson kept a studio on Bienville Street and painted distinguished people of Louisiana. His self-portrait and his picture of Michel Jean Fortier still hang in the Cabildo. The Warburg brothers, Eugene and Daniel, were sculptors.

But the group was probably more proud of its military record than of its artistic accomplishments. It was in the Battle of New Orleans, January 8, 1815, an action that gave Victor Séjour the theme for one of his dramas, that they first distinguished themselves. General Andrew Jackson was the commanding officer of the American forces. When he discovered the British just seven miles from New Orleans and advancing on the city, he threw all the men he had at the enemy, including Choctaw Indians, Baratarians and the brigades of free Negroes. The invader was defeated and turned back, of course, and General Jackson, who had invited the colored men to join his army a year earlier, warmly praised the valor of their two regiments.

Yet in New Orleans as elsewhere in the United States, the life of a free Negro was never without indignities and humiliations. Neither personal achievement nor patriotism seemed to make much difference. So the restless and talented young Negroes of Louisiana spent their days dreaming of France and wondering how they could get to Paris. In the states where the English language had always been spoken and where Protestant influences were stronger, free colored people seemed more inclined to think about the institution of slavery itself and to blame it for their hardships. As a result, they were generally out fighting on the side of the abolitionists against the common enemy of all free people.

Among these were strong and influential preachers like Lemuel Haynes and Samuel Ringgold Ward, who pastored white churches in New England and New York, and others such as Richard Allen, William Paul Quinn, Lott Cary, John Gloucester and John Chavis, all honored by their respective denominations for their work in the establishment of churches among Negroes. After Nat Turner's attempted rebellion, the slave states wondered whether or not it was safe to teach religion to Negroes, and some of them passed laws silencing Negro preachers and forbidding or restricting church attendance. But this only added to the power of church leaders in the free states.

Masters and Slaves

THERE were no slaves who did not want to be free. There were no contented slaves. But there were many who did nothing about changing their condition. And naturally there were many contented masters.

Of course all southern white people were not slave owners. Only the rich and the well-to-do could afford that luxury. A good slave was worth around two thousand dollars, sometimes more, and that was more money in those days than it is now. For every master of slaves in the southern states there were nearly a dozen poor whites.

In many cases the slaves were actually better off than the poor whites. They lived in cabins on the big plantation and ate food provided by the owner. They wore the clothes that were given to them. If the master happened to be humane, and sufficiently prosperous, the quarters he built for his slave people were not too uncomfortable. In some special cases, well-liked slaves enjoyed unusual favors. At no time did they have to worry about their job or where the next meal was coming from or how they would pay their rent. Some poor whites got the impression that the slaves had the best of everything, and they resented it. They began to feel that the Negroes were the cause of all their troubles.

While they put the blame in the wrong place, they were justified in their resentment. The two kinds of labor did not go well together. They were bound to compete, and such competition kept the wages of free labor low and prevented the price of slaves from going too high. Either way, the advantage was to the planter or employer, while the disadvantage to the poor white and the Negro remained the same. Naturally there was a great temptation for planters and employers to do and say what they could to keep these two groups opposed.

While some slave owners figured on spending as little as possible on the upkeep of their slaves, to work them to death and to replace them in from four to seven years, there were many American planters who seemed to think that it was not only better economically but also more decent to keep their slave people alive and strong. They also reasoned that it was to their own advantage to develop and use all the skills and abilities their slaves possessed. The results were good enough in some instances to convince the owners that there was nothing anybody could do that these black folk could not learn.

One old master whose sight was failing was in the habit of having a slave boy read aloud to him. This gave him another idea. Since the young fellow picked up English so readily, why not try him on other languages? Soon the Negro was reading and translating the Latin and Greek classics for the owner and, no doubt, brightening the old man's declining years considerably.

Other slaves did the work of secretaries, and some of these were associated with prominent southern figures. A large number were used as butlers, major-domos, overseers, foremen, and skilled workers. They served as carpenters, painters, brick masons, stonecutters, barbers, chefs, bakers, goldsmiths, and cabinet makers. As slaves they found none of the trades or skills closed to them.

Skillful slave artisans did much of the wrought iron work that was the pride of old New Orleans. There and elsewhere in the South they had a hand in the building of many elegant greathouses. Some of these showplaces which still stand were constructed entirely by slaves and free Negroes. Old Melrose in upper Louisiana is an outstanding example because the original owners for whom it was built were also free colored people. Their name was Metoyer. But it is by no means the only one which owes its grace and beauty to slave skills. The same can be said for much of the fine furniture, inlaid woodwork, and carving that ornamented the story book mansions of the old plantations.

An indication of the range of skills possessed by slaves can be gained by reading the newspapers of the day, particularly those that advertised for runaways or offered people for sale. In either case the owners were likely to mention the special abilities of the Negro in question. There are also many scattered references in memoirs, letters, and other writings to individual accomplishments by slave people in the United States.

One of the most remarkable instances, however, occurred near the end of the slave era and carried over into the decades that followed. A blind youngster named Tom was born to a slave woman owned by Colonel James Green Bethune near Columbus, Georgia. Since the mother was a house servant, as distinguished from the field hands, little Tom was permitted to spend much time in the big house where she could keep an eye on him. This is how it happened that he first heard the playing of the piano, and this was the accident that led to the miracle. For Thomas Green Bethune, known as Blind Tom, finally found his way to that wonderful instrument.

Perhaps his mother discovered that a good way to keep him out of mischief while she was working in the kitchen or spreading the linen or polishing the silver, and when the old master was not at home, was to let him amuse himself by running his fingers over the keys. Soon Tom was playing everything he heard. Colonel Bethune began asking him to play for guests. Then he called in musicians to hear the gifted boy. The musicians played the most difficult piano numbers, and Blind Tom played after them, played the great music without mistake and from memory. There was no longer any doubt that he was a prodigy.

If slavery in the United States did not produce a holy man to be compared with the Blessed Martín de Porres of Lima, it did produce in its dying years the miracle of Thomas Green Bethune, the blind pianist whose performances caused people everywhere to wonder. But Tom was too important to stay on a plantation. His master was already showing him around when the Civil War swept away the planter aristocracy and left men like Colonel Bethune poor, but proud. He was not quite so proud as his kind has sometimes been represented, however, for he took the blind genius on concert tours, presented him crudely, and exploited him as few men of great talent have ever had the misfortune to be exploited. Yet Tom survived it for a surprising length of time before he died in misery and wretchedness in 1906.

His story sums up rather well what slavery was at its best and worst and what it did to the character and genius of people, black and white. It debased everyone who touched it, everyone who came under its influence.

Voices

AFTER slavery was ended in the French, English, and Spanish possessions of the New World, the friends of freedom began to work with new zeal in the United States. Free Negroes and fugitives from bondage became more and more active in the fight. They had now seen other people rid themselves of the slave system by democratic efforts, by argument and persuasion, by talking, writing and teaching, by appealing to the minds and the consciences of the people, by employing pressure and influence. This was a more attractive method than the one the slaves of Haiti had been forced to use, and certainly many of those who worked for the abolition of American slavery hoped and believed that the solution would be a peaceful one. Unfortunately it didn't come about that way, but some of the people who helped to carry on the campaign must be remembered.

First there was John B. Russwurm who, with Samuel E. Cornish, began editing *The Journal of Freedom* in March, 1827. This was the first Negro newspaper in the United States. Russwurm, who was a graduate of Bowdoin and the first Negro American to receive a degree from a college in the United States, continued as its editor until 1829 when he went to Liberia to become Superintendent of Education in that little new republic. Cornish, a Presbyterian minister, ran the paper for the next twelve years, sometimes under the name *Rights for All*, and then became the first editor of the *Colored American*, a periodical that lasted four years.

Just two years after Russwurm and Cornish started *The Journal of Freedom* (often called *Freedom's Journal*), an angry man published a book that he had been writing in Boston in his spare time. He called it *Walker's Appeal*, and it was in many ways an extraordinary piece of writing. Born in Wilmington, North Carolina, in 1785, the son of a free mother and a slave father, David Walker learned to hate slavery while he was still a child. When he grew older, he refused to live where it was practiced. He went to Boston as a young man and opened a clothing store. His business went well, but Walker couldn't stop thinking about the miserable condition of Negroes in the South and in some parts of the North. He noticed especially the effect slavery and want had on the personalities of the victims, and this seemed to him the cruellest part of the oppression. The more he turned it in his mind the angrier he became.

A tall dark man with soft, loose hair, he was considered handsome in appearance. But he felt angry and resentful, and the book he wrote was such a stinging attack on the evils of slavery and the hypocrisy of those who tolerated it while professing to follow Jesus Christ, that it couldn't be ignored. Governors of North Carolina and Virginia sent special messages to their state legislatures condemning it. The governor of Georgia wrote to the mayor of Boston requesting that the book be suppressed. In reply the mayor said he did not like the book either but that he failed to see how he could do anything about it. Walker had not broken any law.

When a reward of a thousand dollars was offered for Walker's head, there was no longer any doubt that he had struck a hurting blow and that the slave-holders felt it. The amount offered was increased to ten thousand dollars on condition that Walker be taken alive. His wife and friends advised him to leave for Canada. Walker refused. "Somebody must die in this cause," he said. Perhaps he thought that would be the best way to make the nation listen. At any rate, he died the following year, and his friends suspected that he had been murdered. His bold, angry, and fearless little book continued to sell.

Meanwhile, the problem before the people of the United States grew bigger and bigger. Some well-meaning individuals and groups suggested that it be solved by sending Negroes back to Africa or colonizing them in some other place. This idea was debated almost as seriously as the question of slavery itself. It was advocated at times by both friends and enemies of the Negro people. The friendly advocates took the position that colonization was a fair and honorable way to deal with a situation which had become awkward for all concerned. The unfriendly supporters of colonization simply didn't want Negroes around and welcomed any suggestion for getting rid of them.

Occasional attempts were made to carry out such schemes. The most important and successful of these was the one begun by the American Colonization Society in 1816, to which the United States government appropriated one hundred thousand dollars in 1819. This effort led to the founding of the Liberian Republic.

This small nation, located on the Grain Coast of West Africa, a region previously known for its trade in a kind of pepper called Grains of Paradise, proclaimed its independence in 1847 and selected Joseph Jenkins Roberts, a colored man of Virginia, as its first president. The government which it established was modeled after the one in the United States. The first administration of President Roberts continued till 1856. He was later recalled to office and continued in office till 1875, the year before his death. During that time the boundaries of the colony were extended and its economic condition improved, but conflicts developed between the newcomers from the United States and the natives, and the government came into a period of storm and stress in its dealings with the outside world. In spite of difficulties, however, Liberia survived.

One trouble with colonization, where the Negroes of the United States were concerned, was that it could never be carried out on a large enough scale to really count. Another difficulty was that slave-holders had no intention of giving up their slaves. If they let them go at all, they wanted full payment—very full. This meant that generally the proposals had to be limited to free Negroes. Colonization under such conditions could be no more than a partial solution at best. Still another problem was raised by the Negroes who were intended to benefit by the schemes. Some of them had been in this country longer than most white people. They saw no reason why they should not stay here. They were Americans, not Africans. In their blood there were African strains, but these had been mixed through slavery in such a way as to produce people quite different from any in Africa. Through slavery, too, there had been a blending of the African with American Indian and white European strains. There was now no way of turning back. They were Americans—old line Americans.

And of course the great voices of America's conscience opposed colonization as a solution for the democratic problems of slavery and citizenship. William Lloyd Garrison, the most powerful leader of the movement for immediate emancipation, took the position that colonization was too slow to consider. Slavery was an evil. It was unworthy of his country. Negroes were entitled to full citizenship. "I will be as uncompromising as justice on the subject," he said. "I am not wrong. I will not equivocate, I will not retreat a single inch and I will be heard." In Boston, to which he moved from Baltimore, he started the *Liberator* and began to attack the slaveholders through its pages.

Even earlier Benjamin Lundy's paper, *The Genius of Universal Emancipation,* had taken a similar position, and now many other Americans found that they could no longer be silent in the face of what seemed to them their country's iniquity. Elijah P. Lovejoy was killed by a mob in Alton, Illinois, because he would not stop publishing his antislavery paper. Wendell Phillips closed his law office in Boston and became one of the nation's foremost orators, delivering many speeches in the interest of the Negro. John Greenleaf Whittier appealed to the hearts of his readers through his poems. These and dozens of others cried aloud.

Among those who wished to see the country relieved of slavery were people representing many shades of opinion. Not all were burning crusaders for abolition like Garrison and Phillips. They included quiet, restrained men like the scholar William Ellery Channing who calmly pointed out that the system was out of harmony with mankind's upward struggle. They also included patient men like those who formed the Liberty party in the hope of using the slow machinery of government to bring about abolition.

Sentiment of this kind was not necessarily limited to the North. While the South probably would not have endured a Lundy or a Lovejoy, it did harbor many individuals and even small communities that shook their heads positively when slavery was mentioned. Many of the Revolutionary patriots in Virginia had disapproved, and the "up country" people were generally considered to be opposed to the system. But the planters of the region successfully limited the influence of these elements.

Meanwhile, the proslavery argument centered around one point—the doctrine of States' rights. Its most prominent spokesman was John C. Calhoun. Such representatives of the South kept insisting that slavery was their own business and no affair of the United States government, and it was on this issue that they finally waged war. Others, like T. R. Drew of William and Mary College, put up a kind of old world defense of a human society based on masters and slaves, but it was on the constitutional question of States' rights that the section really rested its case.

The Star

THE hero of the fight for freedom in the United States was Frederick Douglass. Some may insist that this honor belongs to Abraham Lincoln, the wartime president who signed the Proclamation that emancipated the slaves. Others will want to give first place to Garrison or Phillips or Lovejoy. Still others may think of John Brown and Harriet Beecher Stowe, who are yet to be mentioned. All of these were great friends of the Negro and powerful defenders of his cause, but Frederick Douglass was more than a friend and defender. He was the slave himself, transformed into a statesman and leader. He was both defender and defended, the voice and symbol of what the Negro might become.

He was born in Tuckahoe, Maryland, in 1817, the son of Harriet Bailey, a slave. The name of his white father remains unknown. His childhood was like that of any other youngster born in slavery in Talbot County in the early years of the nineteenth century. He was cared for by his grandmother while his mother worked in the fields with the younger women of the plantation. So it was the older woman who gave him his first sense of human affection. Before he was seven, however, he was torn from her and thrown into a house of children ruled by an evil old woman who showed him no love at all, and soon thereafter he was put to work.

Fred's resentment against the system began when he was separated from his grandmother. It increased as he grew older and saw other slaves beaten and brutalized and sometimes murdered. When he learned that he was to be taken to Baltimore to serve another household, his hopes rose, and in many ways the new surroundings turned out to be an improvement. In later years, Fred looked back on this move as the incident that saved him from a life of slavery.

The first step, of course, was learning to read. Even as a child, Fred seemed to realize that there was little he could accomplish without knowledge. In Baltimore he found a way. Through the help of his white playmates on the street, he learned the words from an old speller he carried in his pocket. Through these boys he also learned another wonderful truth. They demonstrated to him that childhood has a better regard for humanity than has old age. In all his contacts in the city Fred never met a boy who did not feel the injustice of slavery. And they were always ready to pass along to Fred the things they had learned in school. By the time he was thirteen, Fred was reading and enjoying the stirring speeches in his copy of *The Columbian Orator*. He was also pondering what it had to say about liberty. This made him even more miserable about his own condition.

In time he was sent to work in a shipyard and there he picked up skill in writing, but all of this ended suddenly. Fred was removed to the country again and put in charge of a rough character hired as a slave-breaker. By now Fred had grown to be a powerful six-footer, and he refused to be broken. Instead he gave the brutal fellow a beating and made a break for freedom.

This first attempt at escape failed, but a second break, somewhat later, was more carefully planned and carried the stalwart, untamed Fred out of bondage, through New York, and into the free air of New Bedford in 1838. Here he gave himself the name of Douglass and went to work on the docks of the northern city. Three years passed, years of steady work without a vacation, years in which Fred discovered the world of literature and perfected his own mastery of words, years in which he read the *Liberator* regularly.

In 1841, he decided to attend an antislavery convention in Nantucket, Massachusetts. While there he was casually asked to say a few words. The occasion turned out to be one of the great moments in the history of the Negro in the New World. The handsome figure of the twenty-four-year-old shipyard worker struck the audience immediately. Some of them talked about it for the rest of their lives. When he began to speak, they were impressed by the rich and pleasing quality of his deep voice. And the story he told of his own bondage and freedom melted their hearts. From that moment on, Frederick Douglass belonged to his people and their cause.

The Massachusetts Antislavery Society employed him to lecture. He became a disciple of Garrison and worked throughout the North and East, lecturing from every kind of platform and pulpit. His manner improved, his thought broadened and deepened. Four years later he went to England and spent two years among the liberals of that country, addressing large audiences and still growing as an intellectual. It was in England that friends raised money to buy his freedom from the slave master who still claimed to own him. And it was in England that he secured the first backing for *The North Star*, the antislavery paper he had dreamed of editing. He returned to the United States and began issuing his newspaper weekly from Rochester. Later the name was changed to *Frederick Douglass' Paper*, but he did not stop publishing it until slavery was abolished in this country.

Meanwhile, his life was not without complications. He

broke with Garrison, his former teacher and guide on the question of method, and Douglass took the way of those favoring deliberate political action as the best course by which to win abolition. He found himself in a puzzling situation when John Brown tried to enlist his help in a plan to emancipate the slaves by force. And as he grew in power and influence, the slave states made him the object of their hate.

When the Civil War began, President Lincoln called Douglass in and consulted with him on questions relating to Negro soldiers. After that, Douglass helped to enlist men for the Massachusetts regiments, and his own sons joined up. He went to Washington when the War ended and for three years edited another weekly newspaper, *The New National Era*. Later he served the United States government as Marshal, Recorder of Deeds for the District of Columbia, and finally as Minister to Haiti.

Many of his orations were printed and distributed as pamphlets because of their wide appeal. None of these quite matched the story of his own life. This book appeared first in 1845. It was called *The Narrative of Frederick Douglass* and was written partly to convince people who couldn't believe that the sensitive and intelligent person who stood before them was actually an escaped slave. When they read the book, they became even more perplexed. They couldn't understand how a man just out of slavery could write so well. A few years later Douglass brought the story up to date in a new edition called *My Bondage and Freedom*. Still later, toward the close of his active career, he revised his book again and published it as *The Life and Times of Frederick Douglass.* Each edition had added new material, bringing the story further along, so that the final book was several times longer than the first one. It is one of the books that should be read by everyone interested in the story of Negro Americans.

Four Who Fled

THE road that Frederick Douglass took to freedom
was also followed by many other slaves. So many
escaped in this way that people began talking about an
"underground railroad." Actually there was not one underground railroad but several, running through Philadelphia, Cincinnati, and other gateways to the North.
Each consisted of little more than a series of stopping
points where the tired runaway could make contacts
with friendly people who would provide him with food
and shelter before starting him toward the next station.

These friends and helpers were called conductors, and the fugitives who came to them had to be ready to give the right knock at the door or say the proper word under a window. Secrecy was very important, because slave-catchers were always on the prowl.

At first most runaways were satisfied if they could just reach the free soil of the North, but there came a time when that wasn't enough. The Fugitive Slave Law was the climax of a long series of efforts by the slave states to have the government of the United States require free states to help capture and return escaped bondsmen. On this point they did not want their doctrine of States' rights to apply. When they finally got their wish through the passage of a severe law in 1850, they were probably disappointed with its results. The friends of freedom in the North were angered by the law, and the underground railroad began to operate as never before. First it was used to help Negroes who had already settled on free soil to reach Canada before they could be returned to slavery. Then it began to reach down into the South, and thousands of others were rescued from slavery each year thereafter.

Some of those who won their freedom in this way spent the rest of their lives helping others to escape. Of these Harriet Tubman was perhaps the most famous. This stern-faced woman had been a slave in Maryland. In her early years she had been cruelly treated. Then she traveled the underground to freedom and began to take her revenge on the slave system. She did this by returning to the South and leading others from the darkness of bondage toward the light of the North Star.

Not all slaves had the fearlessness of Harriet Tubman. Not all of them knew how to fade into a forest as she did. Not all were able to walk on the big road with a straight face so as not to arouse the suspicion of the patrolmen who watched for runaways. Not all could find their way through strange cities like Philadelphia and strike out for the next station on the way. Not all had the heart to walk alone in the big unknown world. Many of them needed a companion, and Harriet Tubman knew that she was the one to help them.

After her own deliverance she made no less than nineteen trips to the South, helping hundreds of other slaves to make their way to freedom. She didn't talk much about her activities, since it would have been unsafe to do so, but underground conductors like William Still of Philadelphia, who kept records of passengers, frequently mention in their reminiscences and memoirs how often that heroic dark woman passed their station leading a band of fugitives. Harriet herself said on one occasion, "On my underground railroad, I never run my train off the track and I never lost a passenger."

An indication of what the slaveholders thought of her may be gathered from the fact that they offered a reward of forty thousand dollars for her capture during the time when she was most active. But nobody collected it. Harriet would suddenly show up at an antislavery meeting in Michigan or Ohio, upper New York State or Massachusetts, say a few simple but moving words to those present, and travel on. Talking wasn't her talent. She was a woman of action, and her work could never wait very long.

Her pictures indicate that she was a woman of simple, if not crude, appearance. Some of her front teeth were missing, and it was said that she had lost them as a young girl on the plantation when she was hit in the face by an overseer. For this Harriet paid back her former owner with interest.

The high mark of her adventures came in 1857 when she undertook to snatch her own father and mother out of slavery. Getting those tottering old people past danger seemed an almost impossible task, but Harriet did it. After her death the people of Auburn, New York, among whom she had settled, put a tablet in the public Auditorium in her honor. Of her they said, "She braved every danger and overcame every obstacle."

Another who could not sleep peacefully while his fellow men were still suffering in slavery was Josiah Henson. Like Douglass and Tubman, Henson was born in Maryland, but it was not until after he had been sent to Kentucky that he made his escape. In his case, getting away was not difficult. He enjoyed the complete confidence of his owner and traveled from state to state in the master's interest. In fact, he was placed in charge of other slaves. But his own welfare did not blind him to the condition of others. Henson looked at slavery from every point of view and decided there was no good in it.

Then he considered the idea of running away and decided as a Christian and a part-time preacher that it was no sin. He preached a few sermons in friendly churches on the Ohio side of the river, raised a few collections, and bought a ticket to Canada.

In Canada he became a leader among the fugitives from slavery who had settled there. Then his mind turned to the relatives and friends he had left behind, and he went to work in their behalf. Sometimes he returned to the South to assist those who could not leave without help, but mainly he aided by lecturing and telling his own story and thus raising money to pay the way of others. He was able to account for one hundred and eighteen Kentucky people brought out of slavery by his efforts.

Perhaps even more important to the cause of emancipation, however, was another result of his personal story. Harriet Beecher Stowe heard Henson tell it and later read the book, *The Life of Josiah Henson, as Narrated by Himself*. She was so impressed she decided to write a novel on a similar subject, using Henson as a model for her hero. The character she created was something of a namby-pamby and didn't actually resemble Josiah Henson very much, but Mrs. Stowe's book became a great sensation. It was *Uncle Tom's Cabin,* and its influence on America was so great that Abraham Lincoln once smilingly greeted its author as the "little lady who made this big war."

William Wells Brown also escaped slavery by way of

the underground railroad. This handsome boy, the son of a Negro slave woman and a white master, made his way to St. Louis and went to work in the office of Elijah P. Lovejoy, before this famous abolitionist editor was forced to leave Missouri and set up his newspaper in Alton, Illinois. It was from Lovejoy that young Brown received inspiration for a distinguished career in the cause against slavery. It was in Lovejoy's office that his education began.

Later, Brown became a lecturer for the American Anti-slavery Society. He made a fine impression on his audiences and won many friends for abolition in the years between 1843 and 1849. Then he went to England and France and met a number of prominent European advocates of freedom, among them Victor Hugo and De Tocqueville.

Brown studied medicine, perhaps with the expectation of settling down to a quiet practice after the struggle for emancipation was over, but the time never came. He returned home and continued to fight for freedom. He contributed regularly to newspapers in the United States and abroad and wrote a number of books, some of which represented pioneer efforts in new fields. To William Wells Brown goes the distinction of having been the first Negro author in the United States to write and publish a novel. Brown's *Clotelle: or the President's Daughter* was a story of slave life in the South. It appeared in England in 1853. Eleven years later an American edition was published, somewhat revised. His books of history were for two decades the main source of information about Negro Americans.

Still another who escaped was Samuel Ringgold Ward, whose parents fled with him in their arms. This couple settled in New York, where their son received enough education to become a school teacher. Later he entered the ministry and was so highly regarded as a speaker that for several years he was engaged as pastor of a white Presbyterian church in South Butler, New York. All the while he worked as an agent of the underground railroad. In this work he was closely associated with Gerrit Smith, the great abolitionist leader of Syracuse. In 1851, however, Ward made a speech that even New York wouldn't tolerate, and he had to flee to Canada. His lectures thereafter were confined to such British possessions as Canada, England and the island of Jamaica, and he was lost to the abolitionist movement in the United States.

But Ward was rated as second only to Douglass as an orator in a time when the lecture platform was the most effective means of reaching the public and in a day when the enslaved people of the South sent many gifted speakers out of bondage to plead their cause before the nation and the world.

The Amistad

THE story of the *Amistad* must be included among
the events leading to a showdown on the slavery
question in the United States. Like the Dred Scott Decision, the Missouri Compromise, and the Fugitive Slave
Law, all of which are better known to most readers of
American history, it belongs with the series of issues
which provoked disputes throughout the country and
centered attention on the moral and legal points of the
argument. The effect of each was to cause people to

take sides and thereby to hasten the war between the States.

Americans in general first heard of the *Amistad* in August of 1839 when the Coast Survey brig, *Washington,* sighted a "long, low, black schooner" off Long Island. Something about the behavior of the vessel seemed strange to the officer in command of the *Washington,* and he promptly sent a boat's crew to take a closer look. When members of the party went aboard, they were astonished to find only Negroes on deck, all of them armed with cane knives. This so aroused the leader of the boat crew that he quickly climbed into the rigging, drew his pistol and ordered the Africans below. Many of them started moving slowly toward the hatches, but while this was going on, the leader of the fugitives, with three hundred doubloons in his belt and a dog under each arm, made a great, splashing leap overboard.

He came up a hundred yards away without the dogs or the doubloons, and a boat put out after him. The dark swimmer, his shoulders and arms flashing in and out of the water, dived and dodged for forty minutes before he was taken. His captors returned him to the *Amistad,* but when he began making a fiery speech to the other Negroes in his native language, the men from the *Washington* thought they had better carry him to their own ship and put him in irons. Then the *Washington* convoyed the *Amistad* to New London and turned her over to the United States marshal. The next day reporters began piecing together a story so tense and dramatic it made newspaper readers all over the country sit on the edges of their chairs.

Actually the story of the *Amistad* fugitives began months earlier in the land of the Mendi people in the British African colony of Sierra Leone. It was a spring day, and Cinqué, the handsome and stalwart son of a chief, a young husband and father, had been walking peacefully through the bush when four men sprang out and overpowered him. They bound his right hand securely to the back of his neck and hurried him away with other captives. He was sold into slavery and then sold again. Soon he found himself packed in the hold of the *Tecora*, a Portuguese slaver of the usual construction, with only four feet of headroom in the slave deck and with the captives chained together in a sitting position. Here he remained during a voyage of three months while men, women and children died all around him and had to be thrown over the side.

The *Tecora* was in the Cuban trade but since slavery was now forbidden in the Spanish dominions, the vessel landed Cinqué and the rest of its cargo at a small village. To this village came dealers from Havana to inspect the teeth, examine the bodies, and bid for the captives on the open market. That day Don Jose Ruiz, a well-to-do Cuban, bought forty-nine men, including Cinqué. Don Petro Montez, another Cuban, bought three little girls. Together, these gentlemen chartered the *Amistad*, whose name meant "Friendship," to carry their new possessions. Many of the Africans were now unshackled, since the transaction made them legal slaves, and the schooner sailed for the Cuban port of Guanja, about three hundred miles east.

But Cinqué and his fellow captives took a different view of the deal that was supposed to make them slaves. To Cinqué, as to most philosophers, slavery was a state of war. Those who captured and bound innocent people for the purpose of taking away their freedom were simply inviting the victims to save themselves if they could. In Africa, defeated enemies were enslaved.

On the fourth night out, Cinqué and his men waited till all were asleep but the sailor at the helm. A few whispered words, a few gestures under the stars, and they had their directions. Their first objective was the forecastle. Here they surprised the sleeping sailors and captured their cane knives. Above, the captain and his personal slave, sleeping on mattresses, heard the commotion. Perhaps the slaves were hungry, the captain thought. He ordered his slave to go down and throw some bread to them. But he scarcely had the words out of his mouth when Cinqué's cane knife struck him dead. Another African rushed in and killed his servant. Still others went to work on Don Pedro Montez and Don Jose Ruiz, but Cinqué interrupted them. He had a better idea.

Instead of putting the would-be owners to death immediately, it was suggested, the Africans might consider tying the two men together by their wrists and forcing them to steer the ship. They settled on this plan, and Cinqué took command of the *Amistad*. Meanwhile, the captain and his personal slave, who also served as the vessel's cook, were thrown overboard, and the next day the sailors were put ashore in a small boat. The *Amistad* was headed toward Africa.

But only as long as the sun was in the sky and Cinqué could check on the directions was the course for Africa held. At night Montez and Ruiz cunningly deceived the Africans by taking another course. They brought the vessel toward the north and west in the hope of finding either a rescuing ship or a friendly shore. They had no doubt of what would happen to them once they reached the coast of Africa.

This strange cruise lasted many weeks. Meanwhile the Africans sustained themselves by consuming the ship's supplies of wine and raisins. They broke into everything that looked like food or drink, including the cabinet of medicines, and devoured it all. Ten of their number died before Cinqué could work out a rationing system and establish a regulation against the eating of anything he had not first examined. Nevertheless all supplies were exhausted, and the *Amistad* was desperate for water when it coasted along the southern shore of Long Island and began looking for a fair anchorage. Cinqué and his men, making an excursion ashore, learned that they were a long way from home. They were still trying to find someone to come aboard and steer their vessel to Africa when the Coast Survey brig *Washington,* taking soundings in the area, sighted them.

The captives were taken to New Haven, charged with

the murder of the *Amistad's* captain, and thrown into prison to await trial. Students and teachers at Yale became interested immediately, and Professor Josiah Willard Gibbs, one of America's greatest scientific thinkers, then a teacher of theology and sacred literature, set about to discover some way to communicate with the strangers. By playing a sort of finger game with the three little girls, he was able to learn how to count to ten in their language, and with this knowledge he went to the waterfront in New York and finally located a Negro sailor from the British warship *Buzzard* who knew what he was saying. This fellow became an interpreter, and through him the story of the captives was learned. Later some of the Africans, particularly the little girls, learned some English, and the public became increasingly interested in their situation.

In the meantime, the city people enjoyed watching the prisoners do their daily exercises on the New Haven green. Cinqué was an outstanding athlete, as his performance in the water had indicated, and the same was true of several of the others. So pleased were the spectators with the somersaults and stunts that they began putting small change into the hands of the performers, which provided the strangers with some of the knickknacks not usually available to prisoners.

While this was going on, the important issues brought out by the capture of the *Amistad* were coming to light. Ruiz and Montez paid people in Cuba to sign false affidavits saying that these captives were Cuban slaves, hence the lawful property of the two men. If they had actually been Cubans, the law restricting slavery in the dominions of Spain would not have applied, since it did not touch slaves already in bondage. But Cinqué and his associates were illegally held, and the abolitionists of the United States took up their case with great vigor. The court battle that began in New Haven was so tense that the Yale law students were dismissed from classes to attend.

A climax of the trial came when Cinqué rose in his own defense, speaking in his native language. He became so eloquent in a language that none of the lawyers or spectators understood that the opposition called for a point of order, and the court sustained it. But Cinqué won his case. Sentiment turned in his favor, and soon the great American lawyers who had been so ready to defend the captives brought forth proof that the affidavits presented by Ruiz and Montez were false. But that wasn't the end, for politicians who supported slavery definitely did not want these Africans freed.

Representatives of the Spanish ambassador took the lead in appealing the decision of the court. President Martin Van Buren, himself inclined to favor the slaveholder in such matters, stood ready to push the captives back into slavery. But the friends who defended them were even stronger. These included such lawyers as Jirah Isham and William Fowler Brainerd, William Hungerford and Governor William Ellsworth of Hartford, Roger S. Baldwin of New Haven, and Seth P. Staples and

Theodore Sedgwick from New York. More important still, the captives won the support of John Quincy Adams, seventy-three years old, palsied, and almost blind.

The former president of the United States had not been in a court in thirty-two years, but he was deeply moved by the case. He wrote in his diary, "I implore the mercy of Almighty God so to control my temper, to enlighten my soul, and to give me utterance that I may prove myself in every respect equal to the task." On March 8, a verdict favorable to the *Amistad* captives was handed down by the Supreme Court, and the Mendi people were "free to be dismissed from the custody of the court without delay."

The liberated captives returned to Africa the following year, accompanied by two workers of the Union Missionary Society who made this the occasion of the founding of the first antislavery mission in Africa. Cinqué himself lived until 1880 and sometimes served the people of the mission as an interpreter.

Battle Hymn

NO EVENT in the story of the Negro in the New World is more important than the American Civil War. But slavery was not the only cause of the struggle. Some historians insist it was not even the main cause. Many prefer to think that the belief in States' rights, as opposed to the doctrine that favored a strong Federal government, split the country. Others point out that the plantation system of the South, an agrarian economy, had found a strong rival in the new industrial life of the North. The interests and preferences of landowning

southern aristocrats conflicted with those of the northern city folk who derived wealth from forges, mills, in-
vestments and trade. Still other grounds for hostility between the two sections have been found by scholars. But
all agree that there was a war, and that it resulted in
freedom for the slaves in the United States.

Nor is there too much disagreement as to the steps
that led to the actual fighting. These included, among
others, an angry debate in Congress over admitting Missouri to the Union as a slave state. Each side had been
trying to increase its own strength by putting the new
states on its side as they joined the nation, and by the
time Missouri came along, the two sections were so
nearly equal that another state would swing the balance
one way or the other. This made the issue important in
Congress. Thanks mainly to Henry Clay, a compromise
was finally reached whereby Missouri was admitted with
slavery permitted, and Maine was brought in as a free
state. An agreement was made to prohibit slavery in
future states above a certain line while allowing it in any
that might be formed below that line.

Like many other compromises this one failed to bring
harmony, and there were further arguments and compromises in 1850 when problems involving California,
Utah, New Mexico, and Texas came up. Four years
later the Kansas-Nebraska Bill, supported by Stephen
A. Douglas, champion of the proslavery element, was
passed. The effect of this law was to repeal the provisions of the Missouri Compromise. Opponents of slavery,

on the other hand, met this forward march of the slave power by organizing the Republican Party, a political group in which antislavery elements could work together. They put forth John C. Fremont as their candidate for president in 1856, but he was defeated by James Buchanan.

Meanwhile, tempers grew hot in both sections. In Boston an escaped slave named Anthony Burns was arrested by a United States marshal. Before he could be put on the ship that was to carry him back to Virginia, Wendell Phillips and Theodore Parker made speeches in his behalf before a mass meeting at Faneuil Hall, and Thomas W. Higginson led a party which attempted to rescue the runaway from the Court House. Several were wounded in the effort, and Burns was returned to slavery. But the people of Boston disapproved so strongly that they draped their houses in mourning crepe and hissed from their windows as the procession passed. Later they raised money to buy him from his master, and Burns came to Boston to live, later serving as a Baptist minister in Canada.

At the same time, a more complicated case was taking shape in the Federal courts. In 1834, an army officer stationed in St. Louis had moved to Illinois, taking with him a slave named Dred Scott. Somewhat later the officer moved on to Minnesota, again taking Dred along. Illinois was a then free state, and Minnesota a free territory, but this seemed to bother no one until Dred tired of the beatings administered regularly by his owner. With the help of antislavery lawyers he charged his master with assault and battery, and the circuit court of St. Louis upheld him in the charge on the grounds that residence outside the state had made Dred a free man. The master appealed the case, arguing that Dred was still his slave and that he had the right to beat him at will. The state court ruled in the owner's favor. But a little later the army officer sold Dred to a New York man, and again the slave went to court on the grounds that he and his new master were citizens of different states. This time the case went all the way to the United States Supreme Court, but the decision was against Dred. Many people were shocked when the highest court in the land announced that a slave was a piece of property with no rights that the owner was required to respect—anywhere.

While these questions were argued in the courts, while Henry Ward Beecher preached to his large congregation in Brooklyn, while statesmen like Charles Sumner debated in the senate, and while people everywhere read and pondered books like *Uncle Tom's Cabin* and *The Impending Crisis,* an extraordinary man prayed to God in Kansas. John Brown's heart was a burning coal. He had seen too much, and he had heard too much. For him the time had come to act.

Back in Connecticut where he was born, he had never done anything important. All his attempts to start a business failed, and he was fifty-five when he went to Kansas to join five of his sons in the antislavery campaign. Within a year he was deep in the work as no one had been before. God had sent him, he believed, to bring deliverance to the captives and to those in bondage. Slavery was sin. God was against it.

His mission was to set men free, and he did not hesitate to kill the slaveholders if they resisted. In May of 1856, he led a raid in which five of them were slain. Then came Ossawatomie, where he threw back a force that tried to attack him from Missouri. So surprising was the force of his blow that the whole nation paid attention. Then he went to work on his master-plan.

He would take a strong position in the mountains of Virginia. From there he would send out attacking forces. These would strike the slave power with sudden, sharp blows, freeing slaves and increasing Brown's main strength with each attack. Thus he would destroy slavery by making it impossible for an owner to count on keeping his slaves.

Brown took over a farm near the region in which he planned to operate. Then on October 16, 1859, he and his men surprised and captured the arsenal at Harper's Ferry. In his band were nineteen men, including five Negroes. Army troops under the command of Robert E. Lee overpowered and captured him two days later, and John Brown was condemned and hanged. But the impression which this made on the country was very deep. To many people Brown became a hero and a martyr. Others saw him as a criminal. Nevertheless, very soon thereafter, soldiers of the grand army of the republic

were marching to the most stirring battle song America
has yet produced. They were singing:

> John Brown's body lies a-mouldering in the grave
> But his soul goes marching on.

Making a New World

The Disappointment

ABRAHAM LINCOLN came into the spotlight through a series of debates with Stephen A. Douglas, who had become slavery's mouthpiece in America. Douglas was a rather small man, in stature as in humanity, but his powers of oratory were gigantic, and he had already demonstrated his ability to sway Congress. Lincoln was tall and awkward before an audience. His voice was not impressive, and anyone could see that he was just a country lawyer. But those who heard the debates went away convinced that there was greatness in the slender, uncertain figure of this man who had started life as a backwoodsman and a rail splitter. They made him the Republican Party's candidate in the presidential election of 1860.

In his youth Lincoln had gone down to New Orleans on a river boat. There he had seen human beings auctioned in the market square like cattle, and he had promised himself on the spot that if he ever got a chance to hit slavery, he would hit it hard. Later, as a member of the state legislature of Illinois, he went on record. When that body passed a resolution which seemed to approve of the mob murder of Elijah P. Lovejoy, Lincoln and one of his associates protested. It was their view, they said, that slavery was both unjust and unwise. But Lincoln was always restrained and moderate in his proposals for handling the issue. He seemed to have in mind a gradual emancipation, to be completed by about 1900, in which owners of slaves would be somehow compensated for the financial losses they would suffer. His method was to deal tenderly with the South on this point while showing an iron fist on the question of keeping the states together in one Union.

Lincoln said he did not believe the nation could continue to exist half-slave and half-free. The slave states threatened to pull out. On this the rail splitter would not compromise. If he could save the nation by keeping slavery, he said, he would do so. If abolishing slavery would help him to save the Union, he would do that. But the Union *would* be saved.

The more determined, or perhaps impatient, abolitionists were naturally a little worried by Lincoln's approach to the question. Was his attitude strong enough? If they were uncertain, however, the South itself was not. The slave states understood Lincoln as well as anybody, and they showed what they thought of his intentions by withdrawing from the union as soon as he was elected. This brought on war.

In the second year of this conflict Lincoln issued the Emancipation Proclamation, the statement which declared that after the first of January, 1863, all slaves in those parts of the country which remained in rebellion against the United States would be free. The next step was the arming of Negro soldiers, but this had already been anticipated by both the North and the South. The Confederate army had organized free Negroes for military service in Tennessee and in Louisiana. And in Rhode Island and Louisiana, free Negroes were called to the defense of the Union. Yet Lincoln expected problems to arise, and while he deliberated, he talked with Frederick Douglass and got the point of view of the Negro leader. Soon thereafter he made up his mind to use the colored soldiers, with the result that not less than 178,975 of these troops went into the Union ranks before the war ended.

Many of the units in which they fought are still remembered by the great-grandchildren of the soldiers. They included the "First Regiment of Louisiana Native Guards," later called the "First Regiment Infantry Corps d'Afrique," the "First Regiment Louisiana Heavy Artillery," the "Kansas Colored Volunteers," and the famous "Fifty-fourth" and "Fifty-fifth" of Massachusetts. Among the engagements at which they fought with credit were Port Hudson, Fort Wagner, Fort Pillow, and in the action around Petersburg. The names of such white officers as Colonel Thomas Wentworth Higginson, leader of the first regiment of freed slaves in the United States, and Colonel Robert Gould Shaw, the gallant young Harvard man who died at the head of the Fifty-fourth of Massachusetts in its charge on Fort Wagner, on the approaches to Charleston, are forever associated with these units. While there was hesitation about commissioning Negro officers at that time, about seventy-five attained this distinction before the war ended.

In 1865 Congress added the Thirteenth Amendment to the Constitution of the United States. "Neither slavery or involuntary servitude," it said, "except as a punishment for crime whereof the party shall have been duly convicted, shall exist within the United States, or any place subject to their jurisdiction. Congress shall have power to enforce this article by appropriate legislation." This was the act that made President Lincoln's Emancipation Proclamation permanent. Then in the years that followed, Congress passed the first Civil Rights Bill, giving full rights of citizenship to the former slaves, the Fourteenth Amendment, which made it illegal for any state to deny these rights to the freedmen, and the Fifteenth Amendment, which assured them the right to vote.

The first of these laws has not often been broken, though instances of peonage have occasionally been brought to light in the United States, but the South refused to observe the other two. To deal with this situation Congress set up five military districts and sent the army to make sure the law was obeyed and eligible men allowed to register and vote. Conventions were called to draw up new state constitutions in the region where slavery had been practiced.

A start was made. Many scholars who have examined all the evidence are convinced that it was a good start, a hopeful beginning. Others insist that everything about it was bad. It is only fair to say, however, that the more the record is studied by impartial historians, the more it looks like a hopeful start spoiled.

Naturally a good many Negroes were elected to public office in states and communities of large Negro population. Their qualifications for office were comparable to those of the average white persons elected from the same region at the same time. Two colored men were sent to the United States Senate, Blanche K. Bruce and Hiram R. Revels, both from Mississippi. P. B. S. Pinchback served as lieutenant-governor and then as acting governor of Louisiana. Oscar J. Dunn and C. C. Antoine each held the office of lieutenant-governor in Louisiana, as did Alonzo J. Ransier and Richard H. Gleaves in South

Carolina and Alexander K. Davis in Mississippi. Fourteen Negroes served in the House of Representatives before 1876.

But an occupying army is bound to be an unpleasant
reminder to a conquered people, and the South was indeed a region of conquered people. It began to show
resentment against the Union army and all its works,
including the effort to establish real democracy among
the people. At first it opposed the occupation by peaceful means, arguing and voting against the measures it
disliked. Later it resorted to violence by a kind of guerilla
warfare carried on by night riders, and secret orders of
masked and hooded men.

The most widely known order was the Ku Klux Klan,
an organization begun in Tennessee in 1866 for the
amusement of a group of young men who soon discovered its more serious possibilities. Its members banded
together to beat, torture and murder Negroes and the
whites who worked with them. By these deeds and by
their burning crosses and flowing white costumes with
frightful masks and hoods they spread terror and confusion.

Many Negroes fled from their homes and started toward other parts of the country, but that was not what
the South had in mind. It valued the Negro's labor and
wanted him to stay where he was. Actually it wanted to
bring back slavery, and it almost did. The North grew
tired of fighting the Civil War over and over again, and
during the administration of President Rutherford B.

Hayes, it withdrew its armies. The reasons for this action by President Hayes do not seem quite satisfactory, as they are sometimes explained, but the result was the same. The states that had given up slavery against their will now brought it back at least halfway by taking from the freedmen the rights of citizenship, as these rights are generally understood.

In some ways the condition of Negroes became worse than it had been under slavery. A slave was at least a piece of property and to that extent he could depend on the support and protection of his owner. Now every man's hand was against him. If he owned property, he was likely to be cheated out of it. If he walked on the streets, he was in danger of being kicked or stoned. He did not dare quit his job nor ask for a raise in pay. If he took his problems to court, he was thrown out. If he fought back, he was lynched.

Segregation laws were passed in all of these states, and this was perhaps the greatest humiliation. These were the laws known as Jim Crow, after a name used by a black-face character in an old minstrel song and dance act. They required separate waiting rooms for Negroes and whites in railroad stations, separate coaches on trains, separate sections in theatres, separate schools, separate restaurants, separate playgrounds, separate parks, separate everything. The laws specified *separate* but *equal* accommodations for each group, but no one took that seriously. It was very expensive for poor states to provide all public services in duplicate, and the idea of offering equality was out of the question. What the Negroes were given was inferior. Often they were given nothing.

What was this freedom people sang about? The ex-slave began to think his deliverance had been a fraud. The deliverers had left him in a pit.

Beginning Again

I F IT seemed to the freed slave in his pit that he was without friends, he was mistaken. He was also mistaken if he thought there was nothing he could do for himself. True, his world had been destroyed, but that did not matter, for it had been a poor one at best.

The first problem was education. In 1860 only one Negro in every ten could read. Even before slavery was abolished, those who were concerned about the welfare of Negroes in America realized that the emancipated slave would have to be trained for citizenship. Some schools were started for this purpose before freedom was in sight.

In the earlier days, as we have mentioned, many slaves were educated in one way or another in order to make them more useful as servants. There were a good many teachers of slaves, some of whom instructed the children of the slaves along with the children of the masters. John Chavis' school in Raleigh conducted classes for colored boys as well as white. One historian has estimated that in the colonial period of our history about one slave in three could read. But later slave owners came to the conclusion that learning was bad for people in bondage, so laws were passed to forbid such teaching. When the slaves were all set free, however, such laws had no more meaning. This was one advantage of freedom that was not taken away when the Union armies retired from the South.

This does not mean that the former slave states approved the idea of educating Negroes. The opposite was true at first. They often burned the little one-room school houses in which classes were taught, and they made life miserable for northern teachers who came down to help the freedmen. Nevertheless a band of New England professors and school teachers continued to work in the region. In the long run they proved themselves to be not only more brave and determined than the armies of occupation but also more influential.

While the War was still in progress, some teaching was carried on in "contraband schools," as they were called, behind the Union lines. The pupils were liberated slaves and fugitives. These schools were temporary, but they continued as mission schools in the years which followed the fighting. Their first teachers were chaplains and Christian soldiers, but the American Missionary Association followed close behind the army and set up regular schools. The first of these was started by the Rev. L. C. Lockwood on September 17, 1861, at Fortress Monroe in Virginia. School was held in a small house, and the first teacher was Mrs. Mary S. Peake, whose mother was a free colored woman and whose father was "an Englishman of rank and culture."

Just two years later the Association counted seven thousand pupils attending regular classes in all its schools. A year later, in 1864, the number had increased still more, and the number of people teaching and helping to keep the schools going had reached one hundred and eighty-nine. They were scattered from Louisiana to Florida, from Illinois to Washington, D. C. So when the War ended, the Association already had a foundation on which to build. General Oliver Otis Howard visited one of these schools and asked the children what they wanted him to tell the people up North about them. General Howard was head of the Freedmen's Bureau, a government agency set up to help slaves make a start as free people, and he got a quick answer from a small boy named Richard Wright. "Tell them we are rising."

After the War the American Missionary Association and the Freedmen's Bureau worked together to start higher schools. Atlanta University and Fisk were begun in this way, as were a number of others. The United States government started Howard University in Washington, D. C. soon afterwards.

In 1871 a group of singers left Fisk University in Nashville, Tennessee, to help their school by going from city to city, giving programs and raising money. Their leader thought that American audiences might like the songs these students had learned. He was not disappointed. The songs were Negro spirituals, and music lovers in America and then in Europe heard them sung publicly for the first time when the group from Fisk toured the nation in 1871. The concerts were successful beyond the dreams of anyone. The singers were acclaimed and honored wherever they went. They sang in all parts of the United States. In many places, audiences were so impressed that they were reluctant to let the group leave, even when the singers came on stage in hats and coats to show that they were traveling and had no time for more encores. Books were written about the singers and their songs. People showered them with gifts. In England, Queen Victoria engaged her own portrait painter to make a beautiful life-size painting of the group.

Enough money was raised by these singers to build Jubilee Hall on the campus at Fisk. This building was dedicated in 1873. At that time it was one of the best educational buildings in the South. It had been built entirely by songs—the songs of a people just out of slavery.

The success of the Fisk singers marked an important

moment in the story of the Negro. Jubilee Hall became a symbol of the desires of these young people for the highest and the best instruction in the arts and the sciences at a time when some people thought they should have been satisfied with less. It has had a strong influence on much of the music that has been composed in this country since then.

Working with the Hands

THE time of surprises had now come. The state of
Alabama gave a charter for a school in which colored
teachers could be trained. Its legislature set aside two
thousand dollars a year to pay the instructors in the
school. Of course this was not much, and the chances
were that nothing at all would come of it, for there was
no one around to organize such a school and no place in
which it could be held. The surprise was that a white
banker and a Negro shoemaker talked the problem over
and decided to do something about it together. They

wrote a letter which both of them signed. This was the letter that started Tuskegee.

The other side of the story, which was just as important, went back a few years earlier. It began in Franklin County, Virginia, where a slave boy called Booker was born about four years before the War. There was nothing unusual about this boy's life in slavery. He was born in a cabin with a dirt floor and a roof that leaked. His mother was a cook in the big house. His father was a white man —name unknown. He and his half brothers and sisters slept on filthy rags. Their food was whatever they could find to eat, sometimes stuff intended for the hogs.

After the emancipation most of the slaves in Franklin County hurried away, not knowing where they were going or what they would do. When they found that freedom was not all they had imagined, they came creeping back, hungry and disappointed, and took jobs for small pay on the same plantations they had left. Booker's mother and stepfather used better judgment. They moved to the Kanawha Valley in West Virginia, where there was work in the salt furnaces. By the time he was ten, Booker was employed.

A school for colored children was started nearby, but Booker was too poor to attend. He had to make arrangements with the teacher, a Negro veteran of the Union Army, to give him lessons at night. Later, by working at the furnaces before and after school, he was allowed to attend regular classes. It was while attending these classes that Booker, who did not know his father, gave himself the name of Washington. Later he added a middle initial, which many people love. They would rather call him Booker-T than anything else.

From the salt furnaces of Malden in the Kanawha Valley, Booker graduated to the coal mines. There, in the darkness under the earth, he heard two miners talking about a school someone had opened for Negroes in Virginia, a school called Hampton Institute. The name stuck in Booker's mind.

Then the wife of the owner of the salt furnaces needed a chore boy to care for the garden and the yard. Booker-T took the job, but he found the lady hard to please. When she asked him to clean a room, she meant the floors must shine and everything else match. When his work came up to her expectations, she encouraged him to study evenings. And, learning of his desire to go away to school, she approved of that too. A year and a half after he went to work in Mrs. Lewis Ruffner's yard, Booker-T set out for Hampton.

Perhaps it would not be too much to call the five-hundred mile trip, which he later described in his story *Up from Slavery,* one of the great American journeys. Its importance to the Negro's struggle in this country can not easily be overestimated. Traveling sometimes by train, sometimes by stagecoach, but more often walking, sleeping under wooden sidewalks, working along the way to get money for food, he finally reached the school of his dreams with fifty cents in his pockets. He was a sorry sight when he presented himself.

Before accepting him, a teacher asked him to clean a room. Here, his work for the exacting Mrs. Ruffner came in handy. Few rooms have been cleaned better than the one polished by Booker-T at Hampton in 1872. When the teacher took her clean white handkerchief and tried to find dust, she could scarcely believe her eyes. There was none to be found.

In three years this anxious, eager boy who entered Hampton Institute at the age of seventeen, was back in Malden teaching others. Three years later he was back at Hampton in charge of the dormitory for Indian students. He had been working at Hampton another three years when General Samuel Chapman Armstrong, principal of the institution, received the letter from George W. Campbell and Lewis Adams, the banker and shoemaker in the little town of Tuskegee.

The request they made was for General Armstrong, who had done so well at Hampton, to recommend someone to start the same kind of training school in Alabama. They took it for granted that he would suggest the name of some white person like himself. But the general had to tell them that he didn't know anybody who would be available—unless they wanted to take a Negro. If so, he could offer one of Hampton's own graduates, Booker T. Washington.

To the two men in Tuskegee, Booker-T was more than acceptable. Lean and eager and twenty-five, he reached Tuskegee in May of 1881 and started his school in a chicken house. People liked him and believed in him, and the school grew. When he asked them for money to buy an old plantation and to help put up new buildings, they gave it to him gladly. Those who did not have money sent him fresh eggs, pigs, whatever they owned. Tuskegee grew rapidly.

But Booker-T was not just building a school. He knew how it felt to sleep on the ground and to work on an empty stomach, and his aim was to find a way of improving the condition of his people. One way to accomplish this, he thought, was to teach the children of the slaves useful skills and trades. English, history and the arts were good in their places, but he was concerned with the man "furthest down." This fellow needed to know how to use his hands. He would benefit more from a knowledge of bricklaying than from the study of Latin.

This was the key to his thinking. He made Tuskegee a school where this idea was carried out, and he trained teachers to go out and teach others that there is nothing finer than to work with the hands. He believed that this was how the Negro should work his way up—beginning at the bottom. To win the support of white people of the South, especially those who had turned their anger on the Negroes in the years following the War, he accepted the position they had assigned to his people and did not ask for the full rights of citizenship. The time had come to make peace. He was willing to be humble and swallow his pride if that would help. There was work to do that could not be done in an atmosphere of controversy.

As Tuskegee grew and the need for money increased,

Booker-T traveled about, making speeches in its interest. No matter where he went, he was careful not to criticize the South, and eventually the South took notice of this. In 1895 he was asked to speak at the Cotton States and International Exposition in Atlanta, Georgia. This was a most unusual invitation, and some southerners were not entirely sure that it was a wise move. A Negro leader, speaking as the representative of his people in the South, might easily say things embarrassing to the region. The fact that the audience would represent all parts of the nation as well as foreign nations made the arrangement doubly dangerous.

Booker-T was also disturbed as the time approached. But when he took the platform, all fears were banished. He calmed the troubled South by accepting for the Negroes of the nation the blame for the disorders in the region after the War. The Negro had started at the top instead of the bottom, he said. It had been a mistake for him to aspire to political office. Now his people must learn that "there is as much dignity in tilling the fields as in writing a poem."

The climax of his address came when he said, speaking of Negroes and whites in the South, "In all things that are purely social we can be as separate as the fingers, yet one as the hand in all things essential to mutual progress."

His hearers became almost delirious in their approval. Booker T. Washington became famous. Lecture bureaus offered him large sums of money to speak for them.

Nearly every word he uttered publicly was quoted. He was frequently called upon to advise in national matters pertaining to Negroes. Substantial gifts flowed into his school. Celebrated people from all over the world came to visit the institution he had founded.

In the following year Booker-T again made history. Few people noticed it at the time, and even he was unaware that he had done anything remarkable. About thirty or forty years later, however, the whole nation realized the importance of his decision to make George Washington Carver head of Tuskegee's agricultural department. Part of the Tuskegee idea was to teach people to cultivate the soil in the best possible way. Carver taught them to save the land by rotating crops. By discovering hundreds of new values in peanuts and sweet potatoes and other humble products, he showed the South how to save itself from the harmful results of cultivating only cotton in the region. By bringing this unusual man to Alabama and by encouraging his work, Booker-T made a contribution to America that may yet outshine all his other achievements.

His great Atlanta triumph, and all that it stood for, becomes less impressive as we look at it now. Booker-T's words in that address, coming from the recognized leader of his people in the United States, had the effect of a bargain made between the colored and the white people of the South. Certainly the times called for mutual understanding, and Booker-T's proposition sounded something like this: "We will accept the condition you have made for us. We will not try to vote nor take part in government or politics. We will accept the humiliation of Jim Crow. We will be your partners and work with you just the same. In return we ask that you let us learn skills and trades and make our own lives peacefully in our own communities."

The approval of these terms by the South and the nation was almost unanimous, and no one doubts that all parties concerned meant to live by the bargain. Even those who thought from the first that the arrangement was not right—and there were a few—still look upon Booker-T as a statesman for his ability to find a platform agreeable to so large a part of the country in that time of conflict and bad feeling. The sad fact is that the bargain was not kept.

Lynchings increased and reached the highest point during the days of Booker-T's leadership. Jim Crow became more and more widespread. Negroes were squeezed out of more jobs than at any other time. The number of colored farm owners grew smaller, and the number of share croppers or tenants increased. Thoughtful Negroes began to wonder whether or not Booker-T's agreement was a sound basis for modern, civilized living.

Perhaps the leader himself was doubtful. There are those who say that he was tempted at times to speak out against the injustice and cruelty suffered by his people, but he restrained himself. He was sure that nothing he could say would help. On the other hand it might spoil the positive part of his work at Tuskegee and at the other institutions modeled after Tuskegee.

Meanwhile the school grew. It was like a small town, and the responsibility for raising the money to keep it going was great. Booker-T was on the road most of the time. Huge gifts continued to come in, but the work was heavy and the cares were great. And perhaps the worst part of it was that the man who had to carry the load had to travel under difficulties. He couldn't stop at hotels in most of the cities he visited because these would not accept Negroes. He was often unable to get proper food. He broke down on one of these speaking trips in 1915 and died the day after he returned to Tuskegee. But already a new leader was speaking for his people.

The Talented Tenth

IN THE summer of 1894 a young man of twenty-six, a natural scholar and an aristocrat in appearance, returned to the United States wearing gloves and carrying a cane like the German university students among whom he had just spent two years. Fisk and Harvard had given him degrees before he went abroad, and in each place his professors had marked him as one of the brightest of the bright. As a student he had written brilliantly for the *Fisk Herald*. At Harvard, he had won highest awards. Twenty years of attending schools in America and Europe had been a series of triumphs for W. E. Burghardt Du Bois. Now he was ready for a job.

In quick succession he received offers from Wilberforce University in Ohio and Lincoln Institute in Missouri. Then came a telegram from Tuskegee: "Can give mathematics if terms suit. Will you accept. Booker T. Washington." But Du Bois had already accepted the first offer. He never went to Tuskegee as a teacher. Nevertheless, his name became associated in another way with that of its distinguished founder. Du Bois saw the South and the condition of the Negro in America through different eyes, and the program he offered his people was unlike the plan laid down by Booker T. Washington. In some ways, the two were in conflict.

To say that Du Bois was against teaching young people to work with their hands or that Washington opposed higher education for Negroes would be completely false, but it is true that the two men put the stress in different places. Washington thought that much of the liberal arts and scientific work in colleges was an ornament which could wait till the Negro was better off economically. Du Bois was convinced that a tenth of the most talented youth of his people should be trained right away to serve as leaders. Otherwise the millions of Negroes in the United States would have to look elsewhere for leadership, and this outside leadership might not always have their welfare at heart. Higher education was not an ornament for this group. It was necessary. It could not wait.

More complicated differences were to arise later.

Meanwhile Du Bois went to work at Wilberforce. He also turned in the thesis he had been writing for his Ph.D. degree at Harvard, and it is now interesting to observe that the degree was awarded in the same year that Booker T. Washington made his famous Atlanta speech. A year later, the thesis, *The Suppression of the African Slave-trade in the United States of America, 1638–1870,* was published as the first book in a series of the Harvard Historical Studies. This was an honor that would have delighted most young scholars.

A quiet, thoughtful book doesn't make news like an exciting address before a tense audience, however. The scholar's work is slow, and the books he produces often have to be read a little at a time. His facts must be examined, his reasoning considered. Shouting and cheering have no part in this kind of work. The attitudes of people and their prejudices are not supposed to matter. The only aim is to find the truth.

It may have been partly because Du Bois had chosen this method that the country paid less attention to him than to Washington in those days. Yet it cannot be denied that what he said and wrote was also less pleasing to people who had been led to blame Negroes for the troubles of the South. In 1897 he was asked to speak at the forty-second meeting of the American Academy of Political and Social Sciences in Philadelphia. Here he calmly outlined a plan of study which he thought would be worthwhile. Many things were being said and believed about Negroes in the United States, causing more and more strife. Cruelty was so common as to go almost unnoticed. What about the ideas behind all this, Du Bois asked. Would it not be a good plan to study the question first and find out just what was true?

Some people thought Negroes caused crime waves. Was that a fact? Others were horrified by the slums in which many of these people lived. Would it be out of place to ask just how many actually live this way, and why? Still others were troubled about the looks of Negroes. They seemed so different. Would it not be interesting to examine colored people closely and find out how they were different? What one discovered in answer to these questions would help him to know what to do about them. Wasn't that reasonable?

The young Du Bois, back from happy student days abroad, cheered and encouraged by his scholastic successes, dedicated himself to finding the answers. He had completed two years at Wilberforce when the University of Pennsylvania employed him to make a study of the Negro in Philadelphia. With very little money and with no help the young scholar went about the task. His work was so complete that the finished report filled a book of more than five hundred pages. It was so careful and correct that it is still respected and read with interest after fifty years. The most important part of the work was what it revealed. Du Bois showed in the *Philadelphia Negro* that as a people the Negroes were what conditions in the city made them. Yet they were not discouraged. They were a struggling, hopeful group.

From the University of Pennsylvania Du Bois went to Atlanta University and continued scientifically to study the condition of Negroes in the United States by examining certain communities closely by analyzing their efforts in business and by looking at the professions which members of the group had entered. He and his assistants made sixteen of these studies in his span of years at Atlanta. During this time the name of W. E. B. Du Bois became familiar to readers of the *Atlantic Monthly* and other national magazines. His essays were extremely well-written, and *The Souls of Black Folks,* the book in which they were collected in 1903, made a deep impression. It is still a book to be read by all who are interested in the story of the Negro. It comes after Frederick Douglass' *Autobiography* and Booker T. Washington's *Up from Slavery* and represents the next step forward.

We have said that while Booker T. Washington was offering to accept a humble place for his people in return for a chance to work and own homes and live at peace, many conditions grew worse. We must also add that while Du Bois was studying the problem as a sociologist at Atlanta in the first decade of this century, nothing improved. Du Bois himself was one of the first to notice this fact. Negroes were still being tortured and killed without the protection of the law. More and more Jim Crow laws were being passed. Some of the ordinances by which Southern cities require separation of colored people from white in streetcars, for example, were passed as late as 1909.

Du Bois had been at Atlanta for a year when the Democrats of Wilmington, North Carolina, decided to permit no more Negroes to vote. To carry out their plan, members of the party dressed themselves in red shirts and patrolled the streets. One of the reasons behind their action was that the editor of the Negro newspaper had published an answer to a woman who had just defended the practice of lynching.

Naturally the Negroes decided against going to the polls, and the election day passed quietly. But that did not satisfy the red shirts. The next day they stormed and destroyed the printing office of the Negro paper, killed nine Negroes, and drove several disapproving white people out of the city. Many other unreported deaths were believed to have occurred. In some places the incident was brushed aside as of little importance.

The climax of that whole violent period came in Atlanta in 1906. Here again the deepest cause seemed to be the determination of politicians to keep Negroes from voting. An atmosphere of hatred was created by ugly newspaper stories. The rest followed easily. Rough characters started fighting on a Saturday night. Others roamed the streets, attacking Negroes at random. Nearly twenty died that night, and many others were injured. The fighting continued for several days.

Du Bois was in Atlanta when this happened. If he needed more evidence that study alone was not enough, this was it. Public opinion must be aroused to stop such conflicts. Friends of good government, of decency and right must work together. Negroes must put their strength together and use it where it would count. They must win the support of white people of good will. Neither cringing with hat in hand, nor study in an ivory tower had done anything to stop this terror. The time for action had come.

These were the conditions and the events that led to the organization of the National Association for the Advancement of Colored People. Du Bois left Atlanta to become director of its publicity and research in 1910. Already the organization had announced its aim; to "make eleven million Americans physically free from peonage, mentally free from ignorance, politically free from disfranchisement, and socially free from insult." A monthly magazine, the *Crisis*, was started with Du Bois as its editor. In a short time, the membership of the Association reached one hundred thousand and the *Crisis* became, even more than Booker T. Washington, the voice of the Negro people in the United States.

Purposeful men gave the Association their support. One of these was Moorfield Storey, a Boston lawyer who had once been secretary to Charles Sumner. Storey served the organization as its president for the rest of his life. Associated with him from the beginning was the literary scholar, J. E. Spingarn, who became its second president. With these men at its head and a host of others supporting and cooperating, the NAACP took its fight to the courts and began to get decisions favorable to Negroes. Equally important, it kept the public informed and alert as to what was happening. Very soon its influence began to be felt, and the backward drift of events was slowed down and then halted. Then, gradually, ever so little at first, a forward motion was noticed.

When Booker T. Washington died in 1915, Du Bois was already a leader, counted on by Negro Americans. It was to him that they looked when the first World War broke out. What should a people who had been lynched and tortured and cheated and humiliated do when the country which has denied them the full rights of citizenship goes to war? Should they draw back and do what they could to hinder that country's efforts? Should they take an indifferent attitude, doing what they were told to do but nothing more? There was no doubt that Negroes were confused, especially those who remembered Atlanta and Wilmington and other similar experiences. They waited for Du Bois to give them the word.

He did not disappoint them. The word he gave became, for many Negroes, one of the great experiences of their lives. "Close Ranks," he said. Then he explained that the kind of civilization Germany represented at that time would make of our world a place on which all hopes would be crushed. No matter what had happened in the United States, the Negro had more to gain in a world where democracy was at least an ideal toward which to strive.

With that in their ears, Negro soldiers went to France eagerly. And the first American soldiers to win the *Croix de Guerre* in that struggle were Henry Johnson and

Needham Roberts. These two Negroes routed more than twenty Germans who raided the post at which they were stationed. There had never been anything half-hearted about the patriotism of Negro Americans, and Du Bois had told them just what they wanted to hear.

Awakening

EVEN during slavery, Negroes of special talent were
occasionally observed, as we indicated in the case of
Blind Tom, the pianist. An even greater success in the
arts was made by Ira Aldridge, an actor whose performances of Othello were especially pleasing abroad. The
sovereigns of several European countries bestowed high
honors on him and, in Moscow, university students were
so thrilled that they unhitched his horses and themselves
drew his carriage through the streets.

While no others received acclaim equal to Aldridge's,

many more did well as singers, guitarists, band leaders, pianists, composers, engravers, sculptors, painters, poets, dramatists, and novelists. Two Negroes, Charles L. Reason and George B. Vashon, became professors of literature in a northern college.

After the Civil War, and during the terror that followed the withdrawal of the Union armies, there were a number of years in which the Fisk Jubilee singers and their wonderful songs represented the finest expression of the Negro's feelings. At the same time, however, Americans as a whole were taking great delight in minstrel shows, a form of entertainment based mainly on humorous imitations of Negro characters. Negroes themselves participated in some of these. James Bland, the composer of *Carry Me Back to Old Virginia, In the Evening by the Moonlight,* and *Oh Dem Golden Slippers,* was one of these Negro minstrel men. In those days no one seemed to be very sensitive about the blackface make-up or about the skits which may have given audiences a foolish impression of Negro people. Several other Negroes composed songs that became minstrel favorites.

When Americans learned to like ragtime, the Negro came forward rapidly as a maker of popular music. This was especially true after the folk music known as "blues" commenced to creep into it. Negroes of the South created "blues" just as they had created the spirituals in which they expressed their longing for heaven. Those who had not behaved themselves, perhaps, and who did not feel that they could count on riding in the chariot, sang about the problems that bothered them most. Loss of money, arrest by the police, disappointment in love, failure to get the right letter in the mail—these were the subjects of the "blues." The name of W. C. Handy, composer of *The St. Louis Blues,* is always remembered in connection with this native American music.

Jazz in all its forms is a contribution of the Negro to the pleasure and gaity of modern living. Exactly where and when and how it was created are fascinating questions that enliven many discussions and keep a small army of enthusiasts searching for proof to sustain their individual claims, for there are many cities and many people ready to accept credit for inventing jazz music. But whether this art was born in New Orleans, Memphis, in the Mississippi Delta region or elsewhere, its creators and first exponents were Negro folk, and Negroes have never ceased to perform it with a special distinction.

The ragtime years and the years of the minstrel shows, also the years of Booker-T and of the struggles of the young Du Bois, must also be associated with the names of Chesnutt, Tanner, Dunbar, Coleridge-Taylor, and the Johnson brothers. Negro Americans were following the careers of this talented group with eager interest as the nineteenth century ended. These they thought of when they needed inspiration.

Charles W. Chesnutt did not look like a Negro. People who saw him at home in Cleveland took him for just another lawyer of the city. The fact that he continued to regard himself as a member of the Negro group often came to them as a surprise. They were also surprised, as a rule, when they learned that he had another distinction almost equally rare among the practicing lawyers they knew. Chesnutt was a novelist and writer whose short stories frequently appeared in the *Atlantic Monthly*. In 1899 his book, *The Conjure Woman,* was published, including stories he had picked up in North Carolina while he was teaching school there. Soon afterwards came *The Wife of his Youth,* and somewhat later *The Marrow of Tradition,* a novel based on the riots in which the Wilmington red shirts were involved in 1898. In these and in several other books he proved his ability to tell stories well and to win the respect of critical readers.

The second of the group was Henry Ossawa Tanner. After an early life in Philadelphia, Tanner went to Paris in the hope of developing his talent as a painter. This was not unusual for an American art student in 1891, but Tanner probably had a double incentive to study abroad. Like all young artists, however, he learned that the way to success in painting is not easy. After five hard years he won his first "honorable mention" in a gallery showing. Two years later, in 1897, he sold a picture, *The Resurrection of Lazarus* to the French Government for the Luxembourg, where it still hangs. The painting was so talked about that art lovers came in crowds to see it. Thereafter many honors came to the artist, and his work was sought by galleries and museums. Tanner took his rank as one of America's important painters.

Paul Laurence Dunbar was closer than either of these

to the world of most Negro Americans. Perhaps that is why they loved him so much. He put their world of parties, church, home cooking, fiddle music, hard work and happy courtship into poetry which anyone could understand and which many people could recite. He gave them something to laugh about, and something to make them cry. No doubt they also loved him because his short life was as filled with tragedy as any of theirs.

Dunbar grew up in Dayton, Ohio. After high school he became an elevator boy at four dollars a week. He was on this job when he put together the first collection of his verse in 1892. Not many people noticed this book, but the next one won influential friends, and the third, *Lyrics of Lowly Life*, brought him to the attention of many readers in 1896. Ten years later he was dead, at the age of thirty-three. But the books he wrote during these years of suffering and declining health made his name a familiar one in many thousands of American homes.

Samuel Coleridge-Taylor was not an American, but was associated with Negroes of the United States in many ways. Most of his life was spent in London, where he was born, but he visited the United States more than once, and his Negro friends from this country did not fail to call on him when they were in England. In the same years that Dunbar and Chesnutt were becoming known on this side of the Atlantic, Coleridge-Taylor was distinguishing himself among British composers. He wrote three cantatas based on Longfellow's poem, *Hiawatha*, and these are the works that first made him well-known, but some musicians prefer the compositions in which he was inspired by Negro-American folk songs. Coleridge-Taylor's health was delicate, as was Dunbar's, and his career was short.

The brothers J. Rosamond and James Weldon Johnson, unlike the rest of this group, grew to manhood in the midst of conditions like those with which Booker T. Washington and W. E. B. Du Bois were trying to deal. Their home was Jacksonville, Florida. James Weldon had been a lawyer and a high school principal in his home town by 1900 when he and his brother wrote *Lift Every Voice and Sing*, the song that many groups use as a sort of anthem of the Negro people in America. Then they went to New York City and composed songs for musical shows. But James Weldon gave this up to become an American consul in Venezuela, and later to serve as secretary of the NAACP. Along the way, he wrote poetry and prose and collected books of the spirituals and of poetry by Negro poets in America.

These artists, with the exception of the Johnsons, had completed their main work before the United States entered the first World War, and a period followed in which no important new talents were discovered. This lasted more than a decade, including the years of the war and of the confusion and backward steps that followed, and some people began to wonder what had happened to the creative gifts of the younger Negroes in this country. But in the nineteen-twenties a host of them suddenly appeared in New York's Harlem.

Meanwhile, for Negroes as a whole, there were more bad days in the United States. The War was followed by hard times in the South and the revival of the Ku Klux Klan. This new terror caused thousands of Negroes to turn their faces towards the North and the West, where a good many of their relatives and friends had already gone to work in war industries. Unfortunately, running away did not solve all their problems. They found opposition in some of the places to which they fled, and this led to fighting and riots in East St. Louis and Chicago and in other centers. As the war boom faded and jobs became scarce, white laborers found themselves in competition with black working folk from the southern plantations. The newcomers were not used to large wages and could be hired for a song. This put employers in a favorable position from which to bargain, but it left the laborers of both groups on an uncomfortable spot. Riots resulted.

By this time some Negro leaders were able to draw a few conclusions from the experiences of their people in war and peace, and one observation was especially clear. The condition of the Negro people in America always improved during a war. A war experience not only called for greater cooperation between all elements of the population, but it also broke up old habits and patterns of life and made readjustments possible, generally to the advantage of those who had occupied the more cramped positions. A second observation was equally plain. Wars were always followed by periods of domestic strife during which the Negro was likely to get more than his share of the knocks. After the American Revolution slavery took a stronger hold and the treatment of slaves grew more harsh. After the Civil War Negroes were blamed when Union efforts to reconstruct the damaged South failed. And after the first World War they found themselves caught in still another net.

In Illinois, which was right in the middle of these post-war troubles with a serious race riot at each end of the state, the governor appointed a commission to inquire into the background and causes of the outbreaks. A scientific analysis somewhat like the examination W. E. B. Du Bois had made of conditions in Philadelphia more than twenty years earlier was needed. Among those selected for this job was a young Negro war veteran, back from service as a regimental sergeant major with the 365th Regiment Army Expeditionary Force in France and more recently a student of sociology at the University of Chicago. His name was Charles Spurgeon Johnson, and the report he made for the commission marked him as a scientific investigator capable of carrying on and advancing factual research of the kind Du Bois had dropped at Atlanta in order to become the Negro people's voice of protest.

The National Urban League, organized to seek employment opportunities for Negro Americans at about the same time the NAACP began its efforts to win justice through the courts and legislative bodies, made Johnson its director of research. He went to the New York office and founded the League's magazine *Opportunity*: *A Journal of Negro Life*. As an editor, Charles S. Johnson revealed wider interests and abilities than his work had hitherto shown. Literature appealed to him, and he made of *Opportunity* a magazine warmly sympathetic to the work of beginning writers and artists. It was through its pages and those of the *Crisis* that most of the new writers of the twenties and the thirties first became known.

Outlets seemed important in those years, for aspiring Negro writers met more than the usual difficulties in trying to make a start. By the end of the second World War, however, the picture had changed, and the term "Negro writer" had begun to be slightly old fashioned. It now seemed possible for a Negro American to be simply an American writer, and some of them, Langston Hughes, Willard Motley, Ann Petry, Richard Wright and Frank Yerby, were working at it successfully.

Langston Hughes, already the most highly regarded poet of the Negro people in America, stepped outside the Negro department when he wrote lyrics for the Broadway show *Street Scene*. The drama critic George Jean Nathan listed them as the best lyrics of the year in the theatre. Countee Cullen, a talented and promising contemporary of Hughes' in the days of the *Opportunity* and *Crisis* discoveries, died meanwhile, still clinging to a life-long dream of being an American poet, but still denied part of its fulfillment. By this time, however, there remained little doubt that some of the poets who followed, including Gwendolyn Brooks, Owen Dodson, Robert E.

Hayden, Melvin B. Tolson, Myron O'Higgins and Margaret Walker would be free to write as they were inclined to write or as the spirit moved them, not as representatives of any racial group.

In the writing of the novel, as in the other arts, the awakening of the twenties was followed by even greater liberation. Richard Wright, Mississippi-born and Chicago-reared, did not stop writing about Negro problems, but his searching mind went so deeply into the subject it seemed to come out on the other side. Almost immediately he won an audience larger than any Negro American writer had ever reached, and before long many of these readers had the feeling that they were learning more about human experience in general than they were about the condition of Negroes in his books *Native Son* and *Black Boy*. Richard Wright was telling stories about the hardships under which he and his people lived, but at the same time he was dealing with the roots of things.

Willard Motley, Ann Petry and Frank Yerby dropped the subject completely and wrote stories about American people who were not Negroes at all. It was a natural thing to do. It had been done by Negro writers in Europe and in South America, but in the United States this kind of freedom is won more slowly. Now, at last, it happened here, and novels like Motley's *Knock on Any Door* and Yerby's *The Foxes of Harrow* and *The Vixens* were read like the books of any other best-selling writer. Few people knew or cared, so far as one could guess, that the authors were Negro Americans.

In the same way painters and sculptors found freedom of expression. In the twenties and early thirties the Negro's talent in the visual arts was represented most favorably by the work of Aaron Douglas, whose mural decorations were widely praised, but a number of other painters and sculptors appeared soon after, and people who saw the pictures or the statuary were not always reminded of the racial identity of the artist. In the cases of Jacob Lawrence and Horace Pippin, perhaps, this was not so true, for theirs is the kind of painting that is sometimes called primitive, but in their careers, the new freedom could be seen. The sculptor Richmond Barthé, whose subjects were of every kind, patiently won his way to a position of prominence among American artists and saw his work placed in galleries in other countries. Thanks in part to all of these, no doubt, gifted artists like Romare Bearden and Eldzier Cortor were able to work without undue handicaps from the start, and the way seemed open for others.

But none of these contributed so dramatically to the emancipation of Negro artists after the new awakening in Harlem as did the cartoonist E. Simms Campbell. In St. Louis, where he was born, there were no opportunities for a colored boy to study art at the time, so Campbell went to Chicago as a high school student. He was good at everything he tried, but he did not like the hushed atmosphere of museums and the long faces of people who stood looking at fine art. He preferred the pictures that cause people to laugh, talk, make noise, and that is the kind he drew for the high school paper at Inglewood and the humor magazine at the University of Chicago. That is the kind he later produced for *Esquire,* for scores of newspapers and for national advertising companies. College boys who enjoyed his drawings used to bet one another that E. Simms Campbell was or was not a Negro. When they learned that he was, it did not seem to matter any more, one way or the other.

The emancipation of the Negro as a musician in the United States may be said to have begun with the career of Roland Hayes. He was the first in this century to be accorded the kind of reception, both critical and popular, that an artist of another racial group would receive. In the case of Hayes this was preceded by a long and painful struggle. After college days at Fisk University, with voice instruction in the music department that had produced many fine singers since it launched the original Jubilee Singers, he made his way to the conservatories of Boston and then Europe. When he returned to his native land in the early twenties, the miracles began to happen. In a short time he was rated as one of the world's great concert artists.

In Paul Robeson's rise to fame more of the circumstances seemed to be accidental, for his wonderful deep voice amazed and delighted thousands of people before it had any special training. Robeson's other extraordinary gifts were equally exciting. He was an All-American football player at Rutgers, a letter-man in three other sports and a Phi-Beta-Kappa student. At Columbia University he became a lawyer, and after that the theatre claimed him for a while. He was applauded enthusiastically in Eugene O'Neill's plays *All God's Chillun Got Wings* and *Emperor Jones,* and his progress as a singer paralleled his acting. In each field he had reached a pinnacle by the time America had reached the point of accepting a Negro actor in the leading role of Shakespeare's *Othello,* and his performance in that part made history on the Broadway stage.

The steps which brought Marian Anderson to the heights of musical glory were more like those which marked the career of Roland Hayes. In her case they began in the choir of the Union Baptist Church in South Philadelphia. There she was first announced as "The Ten-Year-Old Contralto." About two decades later, after back-breaking toils and wearying struggles, when she returned from a successful European tour, Toscanini exclaimed, on hearing her, "A voice like that comes only once in a century." And by then America showed relatively little inclination to deny her the rewards for such a gift.

The new freedom, the freedom of gifted people to express themselves in the arts, was established. A procession of new talents began to arrive. In music these included composers like William Grant Still, singers like Dorothy Maynor and instrumentalists like Phillipa Duke Schuyler. Comparable achievements, with due recognition, followed in the world of sports, in politics, in scientific investigation. Scarcely any field remained entirely closed.

Fortunately this awakening was not limited to creative artists with special talents. It was general, and it was aided by great friends who had been impressed by the courage of Negro Americans in their uphill struggle. Outstanding among those who helped was Julius Rosenwald. The Fund which he set up to bring educational and health advantages to large neglected parts of the Negro population was administered in such a way as to encourage states and communities and other groups and individuals to make similar gifts.

Edwin R. Embree, director of the Fund, has occasionally compared its work to the priming of a pump. Under his wise and far-sighted administration, hospitals and schools were helped first. Then, as time passed and conditions changed, other needs and opportunities were discovered. The Fellowship program, for example, aimed to develop leadership by assisting young people of outstanding ability.

Finally the Rosenwald Fund became interested in the placing of qualified Negro teachers in northern colleges and universities. By the end of 1947, mainly as a result of their efforts, many of the best institutions of higher learning in the nation had appointed Negroes to their regular faculties.

In a way, it seemed, Negro Americans were not the only ones waking up.

The Test

THE depression that began in 1929 was almost as disturbing to the pattern of life in the United States as a war. Past experiences had taught Negro Americans to look for the worst in a period of hard times, but this depression was too big and too widespread to be blamed on any one group, and in some ways forgotten folk were actually found and helped forward while it lasted. Credit for this is due mainly to President Franklin D. Roosevelt who became, in the opinion of many, the greatest friend Negro Americans ever had in the White

House. His concern for the common man included them in a way they had never felt included before.

Roosevelt began by setting up a number of special agencies to make sure administrators did not overlook the needs of colored citizens as a matter of habit. The President appointed a number of Negroes to serve in these advisory posts. Then gradually he began working others into established branches of government, and the influence of this was felt all down the line. Competent young Negroes were discovered and used. President Roosevelt also took advantage of the talents of distinguished and well-known Negroes like Mary McLeod Bethune and William Henry Hastie, who later became the first Negro governor of the Virgin Islands. He elevated Benjamin Oliver Davis to the rank of Brigadier General in the United States Army, the first time the nation had given a star to a colored man. The conditions under which General Davis's son became the first Negro graduate from West Point in more than fifty years followed naturally in the chain of developments that Roosevelt's administration encouraged.

At the same time the influence and usefulness of the NAACP increased under the direction of Walter White, an astute and energetic secretary who inherited his mantle of leadership from James Weldon Johnson. This organization developed a staff of remarkable young lawyers, including Thurgood Marshall, Charles H. Houston and others, who repeatedly proved themselves worthy of the tremendous responsibility they carried as the legal

defenders of their people in situations where constitutional rights were threatened or denied.

The National Urban League grew stronger too. In
1905, while Du Bois was promoting the Niagara Movement, forerunner of the NAACP, as a means of checking
the terror of lynching and to win for Negro Americans
some of the civil rights to which they were entitled, two
other groups were organized in New York City for another purpose. They were the Committee for Improving
Industrial Conditions of Negroes in New York and the
National League for the Protection of Colored Women.
Their objectives were indicated by their names. It was to
a joint meeting of these two bodies that a young Negro,
a graduate of Fisk University named George Edmund
Haynes, read a report of a study he was then making as
a part of his advanced studies at Columbia.

Later this report was published in book form as *The
Negro at Work in New York City,* but the immediate
effect it had on the organizations to which it was read
was to cause them to form a committee to work on the
whole problem of a better city life for Negroes in New
York, giving attention to jobs, housing, schools, recrea-
tion and all the rest. While this committee worked,
Haynes finished his studies at Columbia and went back
to Fisk to start a department of sociology and a training
program for social workers. But he continued to be interested in the New York committee and in the work of
the two organizations that had formed it. He kept them
supplied with all the helpful new information he was

able to gather. In 1911 this committee, together with the two organizations which had appointed it, united to form the National Urban League. Haynes became one of its executive officers. Another was Eugene Kinckle Jones. The League received encouragement and support from people like Julius Rosenwald, Mrs. W. H. Baldwin, Booker T. Washington, Kelly Miller, Roger Baldwin, Robert R. Moton, and L. Hollingsworth Wood, and it went to work on the big job of opening new opportunities for Negro workers in industry and helping newcomers from the South to get settled in the city and make a fresh start. The program spread to all the industrial centers of the nation.

It was to the work of this organization that the young scholar Charles S. Johnson had been drawn in Chicago, and the magazine *Opportunity*, which he launched in New York, became its official publication. Johnson later went to Fisk to become director of the work in sociology which Haynes had started and to greatly expand the research activities. In 1947 he became president of that university.

During the depression the Urban League found itself facing increasing needs and responsibilities. Its branches sometimes had to fight for their objectives, even to the point of leading boycotts of stores that refused to employ Negroes. They supported those labor unions which gave Negroes a fair chance and worked in close cooperation with them. By the time the United States entered the second World War and began a struggle on the home-front that demanded every good pair of hands, the value of this effort was established.

Also established was the poise and leadership of Lester Granger, executive secretary of the League. During the war he became a civilian consultant to the secretary of the navy on the use of Negro men in that branch of the services. As a result the navy, which in recent years had abandoned its former liberal policy, changed its attitude again and took steps to make democracy work. The reason behind this change, like the reason behind many other official acts of the government, was not hard to find.

The problem of the Negro in the United States had suddenly become a world issue. Wendell Willkie, another great man whom Negroes were proud to count as a friend, reminded Americans of the smallness of the world, now that aviation and radio had made travel and communication so easy. It was no longer possible to live in isolation. Mankind would have to learn brotherliness or face a troubled future.

Franklin D. Roosevelt, meanwhile, talked about Freedoms: freedom from want, freedom of worship, freedom of speech, and freedom from fear. This last freedom had a special meaning for small nations, subject peoples, and national minorities. No one could deny that a strange awakening was taking place among millions of people in Asia and Africa and the islands, people who had often been rudely treated by the nations of the western world.

What did this talk about One World and the Four Freedoms mean to them?

Many decided to keep their eyes on the Negro people of the United States. This would be their test of democracy's promises.

What they saw in the next seven years may not have satisfied everyone, but neither did it leave any doubt that President Dwight D. Eisenhower spoke the truth when he said, somewhat later, that change is a law of life, and that democracy can and will make possible those changes that are right and necessary. Even before the Second World War was over, one such change took place where all could see. It happened in Ebbets Field, Brooklyn, with thousands of people watching from the grandstand, and millions listening to radios or following the reports in their newspapers. Branch Rickey was mainly responsible for bringing it about, and as a result he has sometimes been called "the Abraham Lincoln of baseball."

Previously, Negro boys, no matter how skilled, had been systematically denied the opportunity to participate in America's national pastime by the major and minor leagues of organized baseball. The owner of the Brooklyn Dodgers apparently realized that this was more than just an injustice to the individuals concerned. It was a custom unbecoming to the land of the free. He made his plans deliberately because many people were involved and complications were possible, but in 1946 Jackie Robinson played first base for the Brooklyn Dodgers.

Few young men anywhere have been called upon to carry more extra weight on their shoulders in a sports contest than this all-around athlete from U. C. L. A. How he played the game and became one of its outstanding stars in spite of the strain is one of the great sports stories of these times. Soon other Negro players were signed up. It was actually surprising to see how many teams across the country were ready to follow Branch Rickey's lead. Long before Jackie Robinson's playing days were over, the novelty of a colored athlete in American sports of almost any kind had just about vanished.

It had not come about easily or without anxious moments, but it had happened. Perhaps it had been helped by the spirit of fair play which is always associated with baseball, but it was definitely related to a series of happenings which marked a changing attitude in the United States.

In 1943, William L. Dawson was elected to Congress from the first Illinois District in Chicago. Adam Clayton Powell became a Representative from the twenty-second New York District in 1945. Both were re-elected repeatedly; and in 1955, Charles C. Diggs Jr. was elected from the thirteenth Michigan District in Detroit. With the exception of Oscar De Priest, who represented the first Illinois District in Chicago between 1929 and 1935, these were the first Negroes elected to the U.S. Congress since the Reconstruction period, and the first ever elected from states north of Mason and Dixon's line.

The very presence of these men among the lawmakers

of the nation had great meaning. Their votes were important. But it was when they began to introduce bills, defend or oppose certain legislation on the floor of Congress, engage with their colleagues in the rough and tumble debate which is democracy's method, that the folks back home and observers elsewhere began to feel that these new representatives were in every sense members of the Congress.

In 1948, the star of Ralph J. Bunche rose suddenly in the East when he succeeded in mediating the difficult Arab-Israeli dispute in Palestine. This was a most impressive achievement, and it startled many people who had never even dreamed that a Negro American, a professor of Political Science at a Negro college, might actually make a contribution to international diplomacy and help to restore peace on our troubled planet. But Ralph Bunche was by no means unqualified or unprepared for his big assignment.

Born in Detroit in 1904, he had lost both of his parents before he was twelve. A remarkable grandmother took care of his subsequent upbringing. At Jefferson High School in Los Angeles, and at U. C. L. A., he showed what he was made of, and at Harvard he was awarded the Toppan Prize in the Social Sciences for his Ph. D. dissertation. At least one of his teachers advised him to give up Political Science on the grounds that there was no future in it for a Negro. However, dozens of American universities seemed to think differently. In 1949 and 1950, they competed with each other for the privilege of conferring

honorary degrees and other distinctions upon the boy
from Jefferson High who had become worthy of the highest academic recognition. The Nobel Peace Prize awarded
in December, 1950, seemed almost a foregone conclusion.
Since then Ralph J. Bunche has continued as one of the
key people in the work of the United Nations.

A significant distinction of another kind was conferred
on William H. Hastie on July 20, 1950, when he became
a Judge of the 3rd U. S. Circuit Court of Appeals in Philadelphia. This was the first time a Negro American had
been selected for so important a judgeship.

Meanwhile, the untimely death of Charles H. Houston,
another outstanding Negro lawyer, left to Thurgood Marshall, a former student of Judge Hastie, the major responsibility for a crusade in which all three had been deeply
interested for a long time. Much work still remained to
be done in the courts of the nation to remove the marks
of slavery and second-class citizenship from the Negro
population.

Tall and jovial Thurgood Marshall, friendly and well
liked even by his opponents in court, began to get spec-
tacular results. Between the years 1938 and 1954, he took
fourteen cases involving citizenship rights for Negroes to
the United States Supreme Court. In twelve, he and his
associates secured favorable decisions, and one of the
others resulted in a split decision. But the crowning decision of this whole campaign was handed down on May
17, 1954, when the high court decided unanimously that
segregation in public schools is unconstitutional.

As important and necessary as it was, however, the decision of the Supreme Court did not solve all the problems of Negro citizens. Nor did the Civil Rights bill enacted by the Eighty-fifth Congress as part of President Eisenhower's second term program of legislation. To many people, segregation and all that goes with it, like slavery to their great grandparents, had become a habit, a habit hard to break. The border states of Missouri, Maryland, Kentucky and West Virginia began taking steps to comply with the Court's decision almost immediately. But in the deeper South resistance hardened, and it did not take a prophet to see that a struggle of another kind would now have to be waged. By 1956 this battle had begun.

Its soldiers were boys and girls, from first graders to high school students. For the hardest job of all had fallen upon these young people and upon their anxious parents at home. It was up to them to hold the line where it counted most, to win the friendship and respect of their teachers and their classmates. Their weapons were dignity and courage, good will and good common sense. It was also their job to listen to harsh and ugly words as they went to and from school and in some cases to take blows. This was indeed a heavy responsibility. Yet knowing what it meant, they were attending schools which had previously been rigidly segregated in half a dozen or more states by the fall of 1957. One might almost call it a children's crusade.

Meanwhile in Montgomery, Alabama, a remarkable

young man attracted widespread attention by leading a non-violent protest against mistreatment of Negroes on buses. The issue came to a head when Mrs. Rosa Lee Park, a young colored woman, was arrested for not giving up her seat when ordered to do so. The Negroes of Montgomery decided that this was the time to stop riding the buses, and it was the young minister Dr. Martin Luther King, highly educated and deeply Christian, who expressed their feelings best when he said they had chosen tired feet in preference to tired hearts. His influence and his point of view reminded many of Gandhi in India. Within a year he had been awarded the Spingarn Medal and had taken his place as a respected leader in the tradition of Frederick Douglass and Booker T. Washington.

While urging Negroes to vote and use every other democratic method to improve their lot, King never let them nor Americans in general forget that at the heart of this matter was the conscience of the nation. It was this conscience he hoped to touch. Upon this conscience Democracy depended.

A Chronology

SOME EVENTS IN THE STORY OF THE NEGRO	COMPARABLE DATES IN WORLD HISTORY
B.C.	B.C.
1700 Liberation of Egypt from Hyksos	1700 Horse introduced in Egypt; influence of early Cretan civilization reaches Greece
	1193 Trojan War starts
	776 Olympic games in Greece
	753 Founding of Rome
730 Conquest of Egypt by Ethiopia	
6th Century Aesop, slave, great teller of fables, living in Greece	
	667 Byzantium (Constantinople) built
	586 Jerusalem destroyed; Jews exiled in Babylon
527 Expedition of Cambyses of Persia against Ethiopia	
	5th Century Hipprocrates begins development of medical science
	331 Conquest of Persian empire by Alexander the Great

219

SOME EVENTS IN THE STORY OF THE NEGRO	COMPARABLE DATES IN WORLD HISTORY
	218 Hannibal's army crosses the Alps with elephants
	211 Great wall of China completed
	202 Scipio defeats Hannibal in Africa
	44 Death of Julius Caesar
A.D.	A D.
	64 Nero burns Rome and blames Christians
	250 Persecution of Christians in Rome
300 Empire of Ghana founded in region of the Niger	
	330 Constantine the Great destroys heathen temples
350 Christianity reaches Ethiopia	
	481 Clovis reigns as first king of France
	597 Saint Augustine goes as missionary to Britain
6th Century Songhay Empire founded in Africa; the career of Antar, Negro warrior-poet	
	732 Saracens defeated by Charles Martel at Battle of Tours
765 Founding of Jenne, prominent African city of middle ages	

SOME EVENTS IN THE STORY OF THE NEGRO	COMPARABLE DATES IN WORLD HISTORY
	768 Charlemagne becomes king of France
1250 Empire of Ghana in Africa overthrown by the Mandingo	
	1265 First regular parliament in England
	1318 Dante completes the *Divine Comedy*
1324 Atlantic crossings from the Guinea coast reported in Mohammedan writings	
1373 The city of Timbuctoo appears on Catalan map	
	1395 Tamerlane invades Russia
	1429 Siege of Orleans. English defeated by Joan of Arc
1442 First African captives brought to Lisbon as slaves	
	1450 Gutenberg invents printing by movable type
	1492 Columbus discovers the new world
1539 Estevanico, Negro companion of Spanish explorers, reaches Arizona and New Mexico	
1546 Juan Latino, African Negro, receives bachelor's degree from the University of Granada	
	1547 Henry VIII dies
	1549 Bahía made capital of Brazil

SOME EVENTS IN THE STORY OF THE NEGRO	COMPARABLE DATES IN WORLD HISTORY
1557 Juan Latino, professor of Grammar and Latin in Granada, Spain	
	1558 Elizabeth becomes queen of England
	1572 Massacre of Saint Bartholomew in France; Drake makes voyage to South America
1573 Juan Latino's first book of poetry published	
1579 Birth of Martín de Porres in Lima, Peru	
	1588 Spanish Armada destroyed by British fleet
1591 Conquest of Timbuctoo by Moors who had been driven from Spain	
	1608 Quebec settled
	1616 Shakespeare dies
	1618 Sir Walter Raleigh beheaded
1619 First African captives brought to Jamestown	
	1642 Death of Cardinal Richelieu
1645 Voyage of the *Rainbowe*, first American slave ship	
1662 Virginia law makes bondage of Negroes hereditary, depending on condition of mother	
	1666 Great fire of London

SOME EVENTS IN THE STORY OF THE NEGRO	COMPARABLE DATES IN WORLD HISTORY
1688 First formal protest against slavery made by German settlers in Pennsylvania	
	1689 Peter the Great rules Russia 1704 Gibraltar taken by British
1705 A Virginia law permits owners to list slave people as property	
	1727 Death of Sir Isaac Newton
1731 Birth of Benjamin Banneker in Maryland	
	1732 First stagecoach between Boston and New York 1733 Settlement of Georgia
1744 Birth of Toussaint L'Ouverture on Bréda plantation near Cap-Haïtien	
	1756 Seven Years' War begins 1759 Battle of Quebec; Wolf and Montcalm killed
1761 Phillis Wheatley captured and brought to America. Jupiter Hammond's *An Evening Thought,* first literary work by a Negro American, printed	
1762 Thomas Alexandre Dumas, father of the novelist, born of Negro mother at Jeremie, Haiti	1762 Catherine the Great becomes Empress of Russia

SOME EVENTS IN THE STORY OF THE NEGRO	COMPARABLE DATES IN WORLD HISTORY
	1769 Spanish missions established in California. San Francisco Bay discovered
1770 Death of Crispus Attucks, first American killed in Boston Massacre	
1773 Publication of Phillis Wheatley's *Poems on Various Subjects*	1773 Boston Tea Party
1774 First Anti-Slavery society organized in Philadelphia with Benjamin Franklin as president	1774 Declaration of rights by Continental Congress
	1775 Start of American Revolutionary War
1779 Haitian units of free Negroes fight with the United States against the British at the Siege of Savannah	
	1781 Surrender of Cornwallis
1783 Negroes permitted to vote in Massachusetts	1783 Treaty of Paris; end of Revolutionary War. Birth of Washington Irving
1784 Death of Phillis Wheatley	
1785 John James Audubon, son of French father and Haitian mother, born at Aux Cayes	1785 Thomas Jefferson minister to France; John Adams to Great Britain
1787 Prince Hall founds "African Lodge Number 459," first Negro Masons in the United States	1787 United States Constitution adopted
1789 Benjamin Banneker joins group commissioned to survey and lay out the District	1789 French Revolution begins

SOME EVENTS IN THE
STORY OF THE NEGRO

COMPARABLE DATES IN
WORLD HISTORY

of Columbia. *Narrative of the Life of Gustavus Vassa* published in London

1790 Indian war in Northwest territory; first census ordered

1791 Toussaint L'Ouverture's career as soldier, patriot and statesman begins

1791 Bank of United States established. Vermont admitted as state

1793 Thomas Alexandre Dumas commissioned Commander-in-Chief of France's Army of the Western Pyrenees

1793 French Reign of Terror; Eli Whitney invents cotton gin

1800 Gabriel's attempted insurrection of slaves in Virginia. John Chavis a student at Washington Academy (now Washington and Lee University). James Derham, first recognized Negro physician, practicing medicine in New Orleans

1800 Thomas Jefferson elected president; Capital moved from Philadelphia to Washington

1801 United States at war with Tripoli, following attacks by Barbary pirates

1802 Capture of Toussaint L'Ouverture by French under flag of truce

1803 Death of Toussaint L'Ouverture at Fort de Joux in France

1803 Louisiana purchased from France by United States

1804 Aaron Burr kills Alexander Hamilton in duel

1805 British fleet under Nelson wins Battle of Trafalgar

1806 Death of Benjamin Banneker

SOME EVENTS IN THE
STORY OF THE NEGRO

COMPARABLE DATES IN
WORLD HISTORY

1809 Negroes of Philadelphia organize African Baptist Church

1809 Napoleon's armies sweep through Austria

1812 War of 1812. Napoleon's retreat from Moscow

1815 Regiments of Free Negroes win praise of Andrew Jackson for their valor at Battle of New Orleans

1815 Napoleon defeated at Waterloo; Treaty of Ghent, end of War of 1812

1816 Simon Bolivar given asylum by Alexander Petion, president of Haiti, and provided with money and troops for the liberation of Venezuela. Richard Allen founds the African Methodist Episcopal Church

1816 The *Ontario,* first steamboat on Great Lakes

1817 Birth of Frederick Douglass

1817 Pirate Jean Lafitte occupies Galveston Island. Seminole War

1818 Slavery abolished in Haiti

1818 Foundation of the capital at Washington laid

1819 The meeting of *Le Rodeur* and the *Saint Leon* at sea

1819 Florida purchased by the United States from Spain

1820 Henri Christophe, slave king of Haiti, builder of the Citadel, dies by his own hand in his palace at Milôt

1820 "Missouri Compromise" passed. First steamboat line between New York and New Orleans

1822 Denmark Wesey's Plot exposed

1822 Gaslight introduced in Boston. Brazil declares independence

1824 Death of Lord Byron. Bolivar dictator of Peru. Republic of Mexico proclaimed

1826 Ira Aldridge makes London debut in *Othello*

1826 Death of John Adams and Thomas Jefferson. First

SOME EVENTS IN THE STORY OF THE NEGRO

COMPARABLE DATES IN WORLD HISTORY

white men cross desert between Great Salt Lake and San Gabriel Mission, California, by way of Cajon Pass

1827 Jno. B. Russworn and Samuel E. Cornish start editing first Negro Newspaper in the United States

1827 First railroad locomotive in United States built at Quincy, Massachusetts

1828 Webster's Dictionary published

1829 Andrew Jackson becomes president

1831 Nat Turner's slave revolt in Virginia. William Lloyd Garrison founds *The Liberator*

1831 New York University chartered

1833 Abolition of slavery in the British Dominions

1837 Elijah P. Lovejoy, abolitionist, murdered in Alton, Illinois

1837 Morse code patented. Michigan admitted as state

1838 Frederick Douglass escapes from slavery

1838 Queen Victoria crowned. Death of Osceola, Seminole chief

1839 Incident of the *Amistad* captives

1839 Opium War begins in China

1841 Frederick Douglass makes first public address

1841 *New York Tribune* published by Horace Greeley. First passenger train on Erie Railroad

1845 *Narrative of Frederick Douglass* published

1845 Naval Academy at Annapolis opened. Texas admitted as state

1846 Publication of *Les Cenelles*, an anthology of verse by Negro poets of New Orleans, in French

1846 Mexican war begins

SOME EVENTS IN THE
STORY OF THE NEGRO

COMPARABLE DATES IN
WORLD HISTORY

1847 Frederick Douglass' paper *North Star* starts publication; Republic of Liberia proclaims independence

1850 Fugitive Slave Law

1847 First locomotive west of Chicago. Mormon settlement on Great Salt Lake

1850 Jenny Lind, celebrated Swedish soprano, arrives in New York. California admitted as state. Parliament House burned in Montreal

1852 Publication of *Uncle Tom's Cabin* by Harriet Beecher Stowe; Frederick Douglass' Rochester address "What to the Slave is the Fourth of July?"

1853 Publication of *Clotel, or the President's Daughter* by William Wells Brown, first novel by a Negro American

1854 Lincoln University (Pa.) chartered

1852 Death of the Duke of Wellington

1853 James Whitcomb Riley born

1854 Crimean War begins. Astor Library (later the New York Public Library) opens. Treaty between United States and Japan

1856 Birth of Booker T. Washington; Wilberforce University founded

1857 The Dred Scott Decision. Harriet Tubman's daring rescue of her own parents from slavery by the Underground Railroad

1856 First Republican national convention. Crimean War ends

1858 The Lincoln-Douglass debates

1859 John Brown's attack on Harper's Ferry

1859 First passenger elevator installed in Fifth Avenue Hotel, New York City

SOME EVENTS IN THE STORY OF THE NEGRO

COMPARABLE DATES IN WORLD HISTORY

1860 Abraham Lincoln elected president of the United States

1861 First American Missionary Association school established at Fortress Monroe, Virginia

1861 Emancipation of serfs in Russia

1863 Emancipation day

1863 Mexico occupied by French. Battle of Lookout Mountain in Tennessee

1864 Maximilian proclaimed emperor of Mexico

1865 Thirteenth Amendment abolishes slavery in the United States. Fisk University founded. Shaw University chartered

1865 Lee surrenders at Appomattox. Lincoln assassinated

1866 First Civil Rights Bill passed by Congress. Ku Klux Klan organized in Tennessee

1866 Cyrus Fields completes laying of the Atlantic telegraph cable

1867 Atlanta University, Howard University and Talladega College founded

1867 United States buys Alaska from Russia. Maximilian tried and shot in Mexico

1868 W. E. B. Dubois born at Great Barrington, Massachusetts

1868 First typewriter to work successfully, patented. University of Illinois opened. University of California chartered

1870 Hampton Institute chartered. Hiram Revels enters the United States Senate

1870 France and Prussia go to war. Ninth United States census shows total population 38,558,371, including 4,880,009 Negroes

1871 Fisk Jubilee Singers introduce Negro spirituals to musical world

1871 Rome made capital of Italy. Abolition of feudalism in Japan

SOME EVENTS IN THE STORY OF THE NEGRO	COMPARABLE DATES IN WORLD HISTORY
1872 Booker T. Washington enters Hampton. Birth of Paul Laurence Dunbar	1872 Death of Juarez in Mexico. Great fire in Boston
1875 Blanche K. Bruce enters the United States Senate. Birth of Samuel Coleridge Taylor. Death of J. J. Roberts, first president of Liberia	1875 England acquires Suez canal
	1876 Telephone invented by Alexander Graham Bell
1877 Union armies withdrawn from the South	1877 Fighting between United States troops and Idaho Indians
1885 Italy makes war on Ethiopia	
	1890 First Japanese parliament
1892 Hightide of lynching in United States	1892 Gladstone becomes premier of England fourth time. Columbian Exposition opens in Chicago
1894 H. T. Burleigh becomes soloist at Saint George's Episcopal Church, New York City	1894 "Coxey's Army" of unemployed marches on Washington
1895 Frederick Douglass dies. Booker T. Washington makes famous Atlanta speech. W. E. B. Dubois receives degree of Doctor of Philosophy from Harvard University	1895 Discovery of X-ray. Indian outbreaks in Wyoming
1896 George Washington Carver joins faculty of Tuskegee Institute. W. E. B. Dubois goes to Atlanta University. Paul Laurence Dunbar's	1896 Utah admitted to Union

SOME EVENTS IN THE STORY OF THE NEGRO

Lyrics of Lowly Life published. Failure of Italy's attempt to conquer Ethiopa

1897 "Resurrection of Lazarus," painting by Henry Ossawa Tanner, purchased by the French Government for the Luxembourg Galleries

1898 Negro troops rushed to aid of Theodore Roosevelt's Rough Riders at the battle of San Juan Hill

1898 Red Shirts terrorize Negroes in Wilmington, North Carolina. *Hiawatha's Wedding Feast* by Samuel Coleridge-Taylor produced at the Royal College of Music, London

1899 Publication of *The Philadelphia Negro* by W. E. B. Dubois

1900 James Weldon Johnson and Rosamond Johnson write *Lift every Voice and Sing*

1905 The Niagara Movement started

COMPARABLE DATES IN WORLD HISTORY

1897 Queen Victoria celebrates diamond jubilee. Cheyenne and Arapahee Indians held council and war dance at Darlington, Oklahoma

1898 Spanish-American War. Hawaii annexed to the United States. Wilhelmina becomes Queen of Holland

1899 Boer War in South Africa. Horatio Alger, author of boys' books, dies

1900 Boxer Rebellion in China. Electric automobile busses start running on Fifth Avenue in New York City

1901 Assassination of President William McKinley. Queen Victoria dies

1903 Orville Wright makes first airplane flight at Kitty Hawk, North carolina

1904 New York subway opens. Russian war with Japan

SOME EVENTS IN THE STORY OF THE NEGRO	COMPARABLE DATES IN WORLD HISTORY
1906 Death of Paul Laurence Dunbar. Atlanta Riots	1906 The great San Francisco earthquake and fire. President Theodore Roosevelt receives Nobel Prize for his part in making peace between Russia and Japan
1909 National Urban League established. National Association for the Advancement of Colored People organized	1909 Robert E. Peary expedition, with Matthew Henson, discovers North Pole
1910 W. E. B. Dubois starts the *Crisis* as official organ of the National Association for the Advancement of Colored People	1910 Boy Scouts of America organized and incorporated in District of Columbia. Japan annexes Korea. Portugal becomes a republic
1912 Death of Samuel Coleridge-Taylor	1912 Arizona admitted as forty-eight state; *S. S. Titanic* sinks at sea. War in the Balkans
	1914 World War I begins in Europe
1915 Booker T. Washington dies at Tuskegee	
	1917 Soviet Republic established in Russia; Virgin Islands acquired from Denmark by the United States
	1922 Facisti under Mussolini seize government in Italy
1923 *Opportunity: A Journal of Negro Life* started by Charles S. Johnson	
1925 Brotherhood of Sleeping Car Porters organized by A. Phillip Randolph	1925 John Scopes goes to trial in Dayton, Tennessee, for teaching evolution. Body of Egyptian king Tutankhamen unearthed

SOME EVENTS IN THE STORY OF THE NEGRO

COMPARABLE DATES IN WORLD HISTORY

1933 Franklin D. Roosevelt becomes president, introduces New Deal

1934 Hitler dictator of Germany

1935 Invasion of Ethiopia by Mussolini

1936 Civil war breaks out in Spain

1937 Joe Louis wins heavyweight championship in Chicago

1938 James Weldon Johnson dies

1938 Hitler takes Austria

1939 World War II begins

1940 Benjamin Oliver Davis attains rank of Brigadier General in United States Army

1940 Winston Churchill becomes British Prime Minister. Roosevelt reelected for third term

1941 Return of Haile Selassi to Ethiopian throne after defeat of Mussolini. President Roosevelt's Executive Order 8802 creating the Fair Employment Practices Committee

1941 Japanese attack Pearl Harbor

1943 George Washington Carver dies

1943 Allies invade Italy. Salerno campaign

1944 Death of Wendell Willkie

1945 New York establishes first state Fair Employment Practices Committee

1945 End of World War II. Death of Franklin D. Roosevelt. San Francisco Conference of the United Nations

1946 Jackie Robinson plays first base for Brooklyn Dodgers

1947 India gains independence. Jawaharlal Nehru becomes Prime Minister

SOME EVENTS IN THE STORY OF THE NEGRO	COMPARABLE DATES IN WORLD HISTORY
1948 Ralph J. Bunche mediates Arab-Israeli dispute in Palestine	
1950 Charles H. Houston dies in Washington, D. C.	1950 Beginning of Korean War
1952 National Fiction Award to Ralph Ellison's novel, *Invisible Man.* Charles S. Johnson given honorary LL.D. by University of Glasgow	1952 Dwight D. Eisenhower elected President of U.S. Dr. Albert Schweitzer awarded Nobel Peace Prize
1953 Howard Thurman becomes University Preacher and Professor in School of Theology at Boston University	1953 Death of Joseph Stalin. Tenzing Norkay and Edmund Hillary climb Mount Everest. Prime Minister Daniel F. Malan's Nationalist Party wins in South Africa. Salk vaccine for polio developed
1954 U. S. Supreme Court rules unanimously against segregation in education	1954 Columbia Universiy celebrates 200th birthday
1955 Marian Anderson makes debut as Ulrica in Verdi's *A Masked Ball* with Metropolitan Opera Company. Roy Wilkins succeeds Walter White as Secretary of NAACP. Death of Mary McLeod Bethune. Adam Powell, Richard Wright, and Carl Rowan attend Asian-African Conference at Bandung. Princeton University announces appointment of a Negro to its faculty	1955 Albert Einstein dies in Princeton, New Jersey. Death of Thomas Mann in Switzerland. Winston Churchill succeeded by Anthony Eden as Prime Minister of Great Britain

SOME EVENTS IN THE
STORY OF THE NEGRO

1956 John Hope Franklin heads history department at Brooklyn College. Martin Luther King, Jr. leads non-violent protest against bus company in Montgomery, Alabama.

1957 The first National Assembly of Ghana's Parliament (formerly the Gold Coast) opens in Accra. Althea Gibson wins Women's Singles Championship at Wimbledon, England, and U.S. Lawn Tennis Championship at Forest Hills. Troops of 101st U.S. Airborne Division escort Negro students to Central High in Little Rock.

1958 Remains of most ancient human found in East Africa. Sidney Poitier cited for pioneering role in *The Defiant Ones*. Non-violent efforts by Negroes in South meet "massive resistance."

1959 High schools integrated in Little Rock, Arkansas. Major General Benjamin O. Davis, Jr. made Deputy Chief of Staff of U.S. Air Force, Europe. Lorraine Hansberry's play *A Raisin in the Sun* wins N.Y. Drama Critics Circle

COMPARABLE DATES IN
WORLD HISTORY

1956 Olympic Games in Australia. Egypt seizes Suez Canal. President Eisenhower re-elected.

1957 Russians launch earth satellite Sputnik. Nobel Prize awarded to young Chinese physicists Chen Ning Yang of Columbia University and Tsng-Dao Lee of Princeton.

1958 Nikita S. Khrushchev becomes Russia's premier. Cuban revolution led by Fidel Castro. Charles De Gaulle becomes premier of France. Egypt and Syria join to form United Arab Republic. European Common Market established.

1959 Hawaii becomes 50th state. Russian Lunik II hits moon. Last Civil War veteran dies at 117. Prince Rainier III of Monaco takes control. St. Lawrence Seaway opened to commerce.

SOME EVENTS IN THE STORY OF THE NEGRO	COMPARABLE DATES IN WORLD HISTORY
award. Leaders discuss union of African states.	
1960 Negro college students of Greensboro, N.C. stage first "sit-in" protests in variety stores. Pope John XXIII names Laurean Rugambwa of Tanganyika first Negro cardinal. Patrice Lumumba forms first government of independent Belgian Congo. Katanga withdraws, led by Moise Tshombe. United Nations troops arrive. Richard Wright dies in Paris. Wilma Rudolph named Woman Athlete of the year. Nigeria becomes independent. Haile Selassie puts down attempted revolt in Ethiopia. Chain stores integrate lunch counters in 100 southern cities.	1960 Construction of Aswan High Dam begun in Egypt. Hendrik F. Verwoerd, South African prime minister, shot and wounded by white planter at Johannesburg, John F. Kennedy and Lyndon B. Johnson elected president and vice-president of U.S.
1961 Lumumba murdered in Congo. Julius Nyerere first prime minister of Tanganyika. "Freedom riders" attacked in Alabama. Thurgood Marshall appointed U.S. Appeals Court judge. Jomo Kenyatta released in Kenya. Nobel peace prize awarded to Albert John Luthuli of South Africa.	1961 U.N. Secretary General Dag Hammerskjold dies in plane crash en route to Katanga. Major Yuri Gagarin, USSR cosmonaut, orbits earth. Bay of Pigs invasion attempt crushed by Cuba. Peace Corps formed by President Kennedy. South Africa withdraws from British Commonwealth.
1962 African heads of state meet at Lagos, Nigeria, and	1962 U.S. astronaut John Glenn, Jr. addresses joint session of

SOME EVENTS IN THE
STORY OF THE NEGRO

draft charter for a confed-
eration. Sir Alexander Bus-
tamante becomes prime minister of Jamaica. Catholic
Archbishop of New Orleans
excommunicates 3 for oppos-
ing desegregation of church
schools. James H. Meredith
enrolls in University of Mississippi, as Governor defies
U.S. court order and two men
are killed.

1963 James Baldwin's *The Fire
Next Time* is national best
seller. Meredith graduates
from "Ole Miss." Martin
Luther King, Jr.'s "I Have a
Dream" speech climaxes his-
toric march on Washington
marking 100 years of Negro
freedom. W. E. B. Du Bois
dies in Ghana at age 95.

COMPARABLE DATES IN
WORLD HISTORY

Congress. Telstar Satellite re-
lays TV programs across
Atlantic. John Steinbeck wins
Nobel prize for literature.
"Mona Lisa" viewed in U.S.
Peter Snell of New Zealand
runs the mile in 3 min. 54.4
sec.

1963 Pope John XXIII dies in
Rome, succeeded by Pope
Paul VI. President Kennedy
assassinated in Dallas, Texas,
succeeded by Lyndon B.
Johnson.

Index

Abyssinians, Arabic word meaning mixed people, 23
Adams, John, 92
Adams, John Quincy, 154
Adams, Lewis, 176–9
Aesop, episodes in life of, 41–3; Fables of, 42–3
Africa, background of captives from, 11; differences among people in, 12; variety among people in, 19
"African Lodge, No. 459," 104
Aldridge, Ira, actor, 194
Amendments, to Constitution, affecting Negroes, 166–7
American Colonization Society, 130–1
American Missionary Association, 173
American Revolution, Negroes in, 94–6
Amistad, voyage of fugitives on schooner, 147–53
Andalusians, occupations of, 32
Anderson, Marian, 206
Anglo-Egyptian Sudan, early history of the, 21
Antar, hero and poet, 44–5
Antoine, C. C., 167
Arab, armies, 29

Arabia, Axumite kingdom in, 23
Arabs, Ethiopia's defense against, 24; Morocco conquered by, 31
Aristotle, pygmies mentioned by, 13
Armstrong, General Samuel Chapman, 179
Attucks, Crispus, hero in War for American freedom, 93–5; runaway slave, 93–4
Audubon, John James, 68

Baba, Ahmed, author, 34
Bahutu, farmers, 17
Baldwin, Mrs. W. H., 211
Baldwin, Roger, 211
Baldwin, Roger S., 153
Bammaku, 32
Banneker, Benjamin, ancestors of, 100–1; contribution to American life, 100–1, 107
Barthé, Richmond, sculptor, 204
Barton, Colonel William, 96
Battle of New Orleans, 1815, 119–20
Batwa pygmies, 17
Bearden, Romare, 204

Beecher, Henry Ward, 158
Berbers, desert people, 27
Bethune, Colonel James Green, 125–6
Bethune, Mary McLeod, 209
Bethune, Thomas Green, (Blind Tom), pianist, 125–6
Black Code, The, slavery in French colonies under, 65
Bland, James, composer, 195
"Blues," folk music, 195–6
Bolivar, Simon, 84
Brainerd, William Fowler, 153
Bréda plantation, 71, 73–7
Brooklyn Dodgers, 213
Brooks, Gwendolyn, poet, 202
Brown, John, 158–60; enlisted aid of Frederick Douglass, 138
Brown, William Wells, author of *Clotelle: or the President's Daughter*, 145; lecturer, 144–5
Bruce, Blanche K., 167
Buchanan, James, 157
Bunche, Ralph J., 215–6
Burke, Edmund, 93
Burns, Anthony, arrest of, 157; Baptist minister, 157
Buzzard, British warship, 152

Caldwell, James, 95
Calhoun, John C., 133
Cambyses, King of the Persians, 21
Campbell, E. Simms, cartoonist, 204–5
Campbell, George W., 176, 179

Cap François, (Cap-Haitien), *see* Le Cap
Caracas, monument to Pétion in, 84
Caravan, routes, 33
Carver, George Washington, agriculturist, 182
Central America, Negro population in, 88
Channing, William Ellery, 132
Chavannes, Jean Baptiste, leader and martyr, 68–70
Chavis, John, education of, 105; preparatory school under, 105, 172
Chesnutt, Charles W., lawyer, 196–7; writer, 197
Christophe, Henri, palaces and fortress built by, 82–4; ruler, 81–4
Churches, established by pastors, 120–1
Cinqué, capture of, 149; commands *Amistad*, 150–1; trial of, 152–4
Citadel Christophe, 82–4
Civil Rights Bill, 166
Civil War, American, 138, 155–6, 165–6; Negroes in, 165–6
Clarkson, Thomas, 93; Secretary, English Abolitionist Society, 69
Clay, Henry, 156
Cornish, Samuel E., editor, 128; Presbyterian minister, 128
Cortor, Eldzier, 204
Cows, of the Watussi, 18–19
Croesus, King of Lydia, 43

Croquere, Basil, swordsman, 118

Crow, Jim, origin of name, 169; segregation laws, 169, 183, 189

Cuffe, Paul, shipowner, 103–4

Cullen, Countee, 202

Davis, Alexander K., 168

Davis, Brigadier General Benjamin Oliver, 209

Dawson, William L., 214

Dédé, Edmond, musician, 119

De Priest, Oscar, 214

Derham, James, physician, 106–7, 117

Dessalines, Jean Jacques, 81

D'Estaing, Compte, 68

Diggs, Charles C., Jr., 214

Divan of Kings, history of the Sudan (1656–1747), 35

Dodson, Owen, poet, 202

Douglas, Aaron, mural artist, 204

Douglas, Stephen A., 156, 163

Douglass, Frederick, author of *The Life and Times of Frederick Douglass*, 138–9; childhood, 135–6; editor *The North Star*, later called *Frederick Douglass' Paper*, 137; friends in England, 137; help given in Civil War by, 138, 165; employed by Massachusetts Antislavery Society, 137; shipyard worker, 136–7; statesman, 134–5, 138

Dove, Dr. Robert, 106

Dred Scott Decision, 158

Drew, T. R., 133

Du Bois, W. E. Burghardt, author of scientific studies of the Negro, 187–8; editor the *Crisis*, 191; essayist, 189; leader, 191–3; Niagara Movement promoted by, 210; sociologist, 187–9, 192

Dumas, Alexandre, 67–8

Dumas, Alexandre, fils, 68

Dunbar, Paul Laurence, poet, 196–8

Dunmore, Lord, 95

Dunn, Oscar J., 167

Egyptian empire, 21–3

Egyptians, 22–3

Egypto-Ethiopian, families, 22

Eisenhower, Dwight D., 213

Ellicott, George, 101

Ellsworth, Governor William, 153

Emancipation Proclamation, The, 165–6

Embree, Edwin R., 207

Epictetus, 74–5

Estevanico (Little Stephen), 49

Ethiopia, Christian influences in, 23–4; history of, 20–5; Italy's attacks against, 24–5; migration into, 23; religious wars in, 23–4

Ethiopian, empire, 21–5; soldiers, 22–5

Ethiopians, 20–5

Fisk University, Jubilee Singers, 174–5, 195, 205

Fouaris, Abul, *see* Antar

Fox, Charles, 93

Franklin, Benjamin, president antislavery society, 92

Freedmen's Bureau, 173

Fremont, John C., 157

Friends of the Blacks, 92

Fugitive Slave Law, The, 141

Gao, 32

Garrison, William Lloyd, emancipator, 131–2, 138

Germantown, Pa., opposition to slavery in, 92

Ghana, empire of, 27–9

Gibbs, Professor Josiah Willard, 152

Gleaves, Richard H., 167

Goetzen, Count Gustav Adolf von, explorer, 16

Golden Prairies, book describing capital of Ghana, 27

Gonsalves, Antam, Portuguese slaver, 48, 51

Granger, Lester, 212

Gray, Samuel, 95

Gregoire, Henri, 107

Gulf of Guinea, 28; names given to, 36

Haiti, Negroes in, 1503, 50; slaves in, 62–5; struggle for independence in, 76–81

Haitian plantations, conditions on, 64–7

Hall, Prince, founds "African Lodge," Masonic group, 104; Methodist minister, 104

Hamilton, Terrick, author of *The Romance of Antar*, 45

Hammon, Jupiter, poet, 97–8

Hampton Institute, 178–9

Handy, W. C., composer, 196

Harper's Ferry, 159

Hastie, William Henry, Governor of the Virgin Islands, 209, 216

Hawkins, Sir John, slave trader, 50–1

Hayden, Robert E., poet, 202–3

Hayes, President Rutherford B., 168–9

Hayes, Roland, concert singer, 205; musical education of, 205

Haynes, George Edmund, author of *The Negro at Work in New York City*, 210–11

Henry, Patrick, 92

Henson, Josiah, author of *The Life of Josiah Henson*, 144; lecturer, 143–4

Herodotus, description of Ethiopians and their country by, 21–2

Higginson, Thomas W., 157, 166

Homer, description of Ethiopia by, in *Iliad*, 20–1; description of pygmies by, in *Iliad*, 12

Houston, Charles H., 209, 216

Howard, General Oliver Otis, 173

Howard University, 174

Hudson, Julien, portrait painter, 119

Hughes, Langston, poet, 202

Hungerford, William, 153

Huntingdon, Countess of, 98
Hyksos, invasion of Egypt by the, 22

Isham, Jirah, 153

Jackson, General Andrew, 119–20
Jazz, 195–6
Jefferson, Thomas, 92–107
Jenne, 28, 32, 34
John, Prester, legend of, 23–4, 25
Johnson, Charles Spurgeon, editor, *Opportunity: A Journal of Negro Life*, 201–2, 211
Johnson, Henry, *Croix de Guerre* won by, 192
Johnson, James Weldon, career of, 196, 199, 209
Johnson, J. Rosamond, composer, 196, 199
Johnson, Samuel, 93
Jones, Eugene Kinckle, 211
Jubilee Hall, Fisk University, significance of, 174–5
Jubilee Singers, *see* Fisk University

Kansas-Nebraska Bill, 156
Khuf, Heru, 13
Koti, Mohaman, author of *Fatassi*, 35
Ku Klux Klan, 168, 200
Kush, ancient name of Ethiopia, 20

Lafayette, patriot and abolitionist, 92
Lambert, Lucien, pianist, 119

Lambert, Sidney, pianist, 119
Latino, Juan, professor at University of Granada, 33
Laurens, Colonel John, 96
Lawrence, Jacob, painter, 204
Le Cap, 62–3, 70–1, 74
Le Clerc, General, 80
Lee, Robert E., 159
Le Rodeur, French slave ship, 58–61; Guadaloupe reached by, 60
Liberian Republic, 130–1
Liberty party, 133
Lincoln, President Abraham, 138, 144, 163–6
Lockwood, Rev. L. C., 173
Louis, Jean, duellist, 68
L'Ouverture, *see* Toussaint
Lovejoy, Elijah P., antislavery writer, 132, 145; murder of, 132, 164
Lucanus, Terentius, freedom given Terence by, 43
Lundy, Benjamin, antislavery writer, 132

Mandingo empire, 26–9
Manley, Charles, Jr., 105
Marshall, Thurgood, 209, 216
Maverick, Samuel, 95
Maynor, Dorothy, singer, 206
Mela, Pomponius, Roman writer, 13
Melle, *see* Mandingo empire
Miller, Kelly, 211
Minstrel shows, 195
Missouri Compromise, 156
Mohammedan, conquest, 29–30
Montez, Don Petro, 149–53

Moors, armies of the, 29; no-
    mads, 31; *see* Andalusians
Morocco, Arabs in, 31
Motley, Willard, novelist, 202–
    3
Moton, Robert R., 211
Mussolini, Benito, 24–5

Napoleon Bonaparte, 75–6, 79–
    81
Nathan, George Jean, 202
National Association for the
    Advancement of Colored
    People, 191–2, 199, 201, 209–
    10
National Urban League, The,
    201, 210–12
Negro, scholars, mention of in
    Mohammedan histories, 33
Negroes, early history of, 26–9;
    public offices held by, follow-
    ing Civil War, 167–8; Spanish
    explorers accompanied by, 49
Negroid empire, 21
New Orleans, 1850, 117; social
    life in, 117–19
Niger, history of countries of
    the, 34–5; merchant boats on,
    33
North Africa, Arab armies
    reach, 29; conquest and fall
    of Roman Empire in, 28–9
Nubians, 24

Ogé, Vincent, leader and mar-
    tyr, 68–70
O'Higgins, Myron, poet, 203
Ophthalmia, blindness from,
    58–60
Ossawatomie, 159

Parker, Theodore, 157
Peake, Mrs. Mary S., 173
Pepi II, 13
Pepper (called Grains of Para-
    dise), trade, 130
Pétion, Alexandre, statesman,
    84
Petry, Ann, novelist, 202–3
Pharaohs, pygmies in the courts
    of the, 13
Phillips, Wendell, orator, 132,
    157
Pinchback, P. B. S., 167
Pippin, Horace, painter, 204
Pitcairn, Major John, 96
Pitt, William, the Younger, 93
Planudes, the Great, 41–2
Pliny, pygmies in writings of,
    13
Porres, Martín de, (Blessed
    Martín), 89–90
Portugal, demand for slaves in,
    48–9
Portuguese, trades, 49
Powell, Adam Clayton, 214
Prescott, General Richard, cap-
    ture of by Prince, 96
Prosser, Gabriel, attack on
    Richmond led by, 110–11;
    death of, 111
Pygmies, 12, 14; parts of world
    inhabited by, 12–13; size of,
    13, 19

Quakers, influence in formation
    of antislavery society, 92

Rainbowe, slave ship, 56
Ransier, Alonzo J., 167

Reason, Charles L., professor, 195

Red shirts, Wilmington, 190, 197

Revels, Hiram R., 167

Rickey, Branch, 213–4

Roberts, Joseph Jenkins, president Liberian Republic, 130

Roberts, Needham, *Croix de Guerre* won by, 192–3

Robeson, Paul, career of, 205–6

Robinson, Jackie, 213–4

Roman, empire, 28–9

Roosevelt, President Franklin D., 208–9, 212

Rosenwald Fund, 207

Rosenwald, Julius, 207, 211

Ruffner, Mrs. Lewis, 178–9

Ruiz, Don Jose, 149–53

Russwurm, John B., editor of *The Journal of Freedom*, 128; Superintendent of Education, Liberia, 128

Sadi, Abderrahman, historian, 34–5

Saint Leon, Spanish vessel, 60

Salem, Peter, 96

Schools, 171–3

Schuyler, Phillipa Duke, musician, 206

Scott, Dred, 157–8

Sedgwick, Theodore, 154

Segregation laws, 169, 189, 216

Séjour, Victor, playwright in Paris, 119; poet, 119; publishes first Negro anthology *Les Cenelles*, 119

Selassie, Haile, King of Ethiopia, 25

Shaw, Colonel Robert Gould, 166

Siege of Savannah, 1779, Haitian mulattoes at, 68

Slave Coast, *see* Gulf of Guinea

Slave labor, in New World settlements, 47

Slavery, ancient forms of, 39–41, 53–4; conditions during American Revolution, 95–6; skilled workers in, 124–5

Slave ships, conditions on, 55, 57–8

Slave trade, 50–5; European competition in, 50

Smith, Adam, 93

Smith, Gerrit, 146

Songhay empire, 26–9

South America, Negro population in, 88

Spain, African influences in, 29–30

Spingarn, J. E., 191

Spirituals, 174–5, 195

Staples, Seth P., 153

Still, William Grant, composer, 206

Storey, Moorfield, 191

Stowe, Harriet Beecher, author of *Uncle Tom's Cabin*, 144

Sudan, histories of the, 34–5

Sumner, Charles, 158

Tanner, Henry Ossawa, painter, 196–7

Tarikh es Soudan, historical work by Sadi, 34–5

Taylor, Samuel Coleridge-, composer, 196, 198–9

Tecora, Portuguese slave vessel, 149

Terence, dramatist, 43

Timbuctoo, 28; scholarship and art in, 32–5

Tolson, Melvin B., poet, 203

Toscanini, Arturo, 206

Toussaint, François Dominique (L'Ouverture), coachman, 71–5, 77; father of, 73–4, 76; soldier-statesman, 71–81, 109

Tubman, Harriet, "underground railroad" worker, 141–3

Turner, Prophet Nat, capture of, 115; crusader, 113–15

Tuskegee, charter for school, 176–7

"Underground railroad," 140–6

Union Missionary Society, 154

United States, mulatto children in, 88–9

United States Supreme Court, decision on segregation in public schools, 216

Universities, 174

University of Sankoré, 33

Van Buren, President Martin, 153

Vasa, Gustavus, freedom purchased by, 102; memoirs, 102; seaman, 102; efforts in suppression of slave trade, 102–3

Vashon, George B., professor, 195

Vesey, Denmark, early life of, 112; failure of revolt planned by, 112–13; linguist, 112

Victoria, Queen of England, 174

Virginia, slavery in, 1705, 91

Walker, David, author of *Walker's Appeal*, 128–9

Walker, Margaret, poet, 203

Warburg, Daniel, 119

Warburg, Eugene, sculptor, 119

Ward, Samuel Ringgold, orator, 146

Washington, Booker T., author of *Up from Slavery*, 178; boyhood of, 177–9; education at Hampton Institute, 178–9; lecturer, 181–4; supporter of National Urban League, 211; Tuskegee school under leadership of, 179–84; W. E. B. Du Bois and, 186–7, 189–91

Washington, brig, 148, 151

Washington, D. C., 1789, 101

Washington, President George, 92, 107

Watson, Brook, Lord Mayor of London, 99

Watussi, athletes, 17–18; customs among the, 17–19; gentleman farmers, 18–19; height of the, 15–19; migration of the, 16–17

Webster, Daniel, 93

Wesley, John, 93

West Indies, Negro population in, 87

Wheatley, John, 98–9

Wheatley, Mary, 98–9
Wheatley, Mrs. Susannah, 98–9
Wheatley, Nathaniel, 98–9
Wheatley, Phillis, author of *Poems on Various Subjects*, 99; childhood of, 98; married to John Peters, 99–100; triumph in London, 98–9
White, Walter, 209
Whittier, John Greenleaf, 132
Wilberforce, William, 93
Willkie, Wendell, 212

Wood, L. Hollingsworth, 211
Wordsworth, William, sonnet on Toussaint by, 76–7
World War I, Negroes in, 192–3
Wright, Richard, writer, 173, 202–3

Yerby, Frank, novelist, 202–3

Zenaga, Berber tribe, 27
Zuni Indians, Estevanico killed by, 49

A NOTE ON THE TYPE IN WHICH
THIS BOOK IS SET

The text of this book is set in *Caledonia,* a Linotype face designed by **W. A.** Dwiggins. *Caledonia* belongs to the family of printing types called "modern face" by printers—a term used to mark the change in style of type-letters that occurred about 1800. Caledonia borders on the general design of Scotch Modern, but is more freely drawn than that letter.